# 97 NEEDLEPOINT
# ALPHABETS

**B. BORSSUCK**

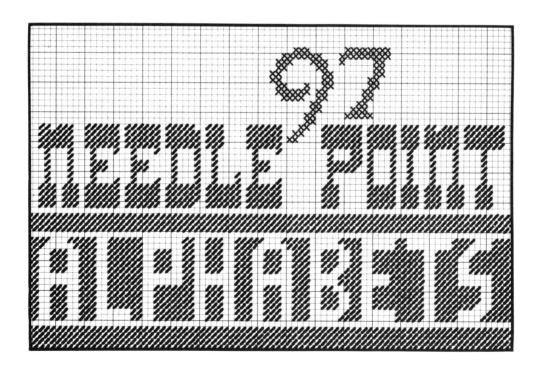

ARCO PUBLISHING COMPANY, INC.
NEW YORK

Published by Arco Publishing Company, Inc.
219 Park Avenue South, New York, N.Y. 10003

Library of Congress Catalog Card Number 74-19792

ISBN 0-668-03723-7 (Library Edition)
ISBN 0-668-03655-9 (Paper Edition)

Printed in the United States of America

The 97 alphabets and 23 sets of numerals in this book are meant to be of practical aid to the needleworker who wants to do her own thing—mottos, samplers, commemorative pieces, monograms—or add, with justifiable pride, initials and date to her handiwork.

The large variety includes traditional styles such as those seen in heirloom pieces, but in preparing these graphs the designer has been more concerned with good letter shapes and pleasing proportions than with historical authenticity. So these are her own adaptations of Gothic and Roman lettering in several sizes and degrees of boldness, without serifs for use in limited space and with serifs for added interest; of Old English Text, Celtic, and Traditional styles for elegance and formality; of Script and Italic shapes for grace and distinction; of block letters for a contemporary look; and of Computer and Blueberry types for a Mod Look.

There are also two 45° alphabets and sets of numerals especially designed for use in the lower right hand corner of a canvas or to achieve a bias effect where desired.

Though designed and executed primarily for needlepoint, as the title implies, these graphs could be used for any thread-counting embroidery.

Two symbols have been used throughout: This is

 for Cross stitch:

 This is for Half Cross stitch, Tent, or Continental

These symbols were preferred over the solid block method because they show the true shape of the letter as it will appear in the finished product.

In one upper corner of each alphabet is a bordered block.

 This border means FOR CROSS STITCH ONLY

 This border means FOR HALF CROSS STITCH (or Cross stitch)

Whereas all the alphabets and numerals could be used for Cross stitch, the converse is not true. Letters meant for Cross stitch but done in Half Cross stitch could have broken lines and open corners. Therefore, seemingly repetitious alphabets of the smaller letters are provided but careful study will disclose very important design differences that ensure good delineation and legibility.

The alphabets are arranged according to size

 This figure is the SIZE NUMBER and is also the count of the number of squares in the height of the letters on the page.

 When two or more figures are given, the number or numbers *below* the horizontal bar indicates there is a matching alphabet of opposite case (upper or lower) in the size or sizes indicated. Thus, if the size 11 alphabet is upper case, there are two matching lower case alphabets in sizes 7 and 6.

All alphabets and numerals are done on 10 squares per inch graph paper. EACH SQUARE REPRESENTS A MESH INTERSECTION OF THE CANVAS.

If canvas used is #10 mesh (10 openings to an inch) the letters will be the same size as shown on the pages of this book. If canvas is finer (#12 or #14) letters will be smaller. On coarser canvas (#6 or #8) letters will be larger.

In spite of this, spacing and design can always be worked out on 10 squares per inch graph paper by applying this formula:

NUMBER OF SQUARES IN GRAPH divided by NUMBER OF MESH OF CANVAS = SIZE OF CANVAS in inches.

To illustrate: The title page design is 55 squares by 85 squares and when worked on #10 mesh, the canvas size is 55/10 = 5.5" by 85/10 = 8.5" as shown. If the same design were worked on #14 mesh, the size of the canvas would be 55/14 = 3.93" by 85/14 = 6.07". Or, IN REVERSE, SIZE OF CANVAS in inches multiplied by NUMBER OF MESH OF CANVAS = NUMBER OF SQUARES IN GRAPH.

For example: When designing for #14 mesh canvas and a picture frame opening of 7" by 9", the calculation would be 7 × 14 = 98 squares by 9 × 14 = 126 squares. So a design arranged within 98 squares (9.8") by 126 squares (12.6) on 10 squares per inch graph paper would be suitable for the 7" by 9" opening if executed on #14 mesh canvas.

The formula still works when canvas has rectangular openings if correct mesh numbers are used. Again referring to the title page design of 55 squares by 85 squares: if worked on canvas that has 10 openings to an inch parallel to the selvedge and 12 openings to an inch between selvedges, the size of the canvas would be 55/10 = 5.5" by 85/12 = 7.08" and the letters more elongated than as shown on the graph.

All the graphs are shown in one color but many of the designs lend themselves to being worked in two or more colors. The larger, open letters were meant for just such treatment.

So, DO YOUR OWN THING AND SIGN IT.

# 97 NEEDLEPOINT ALPHABETS

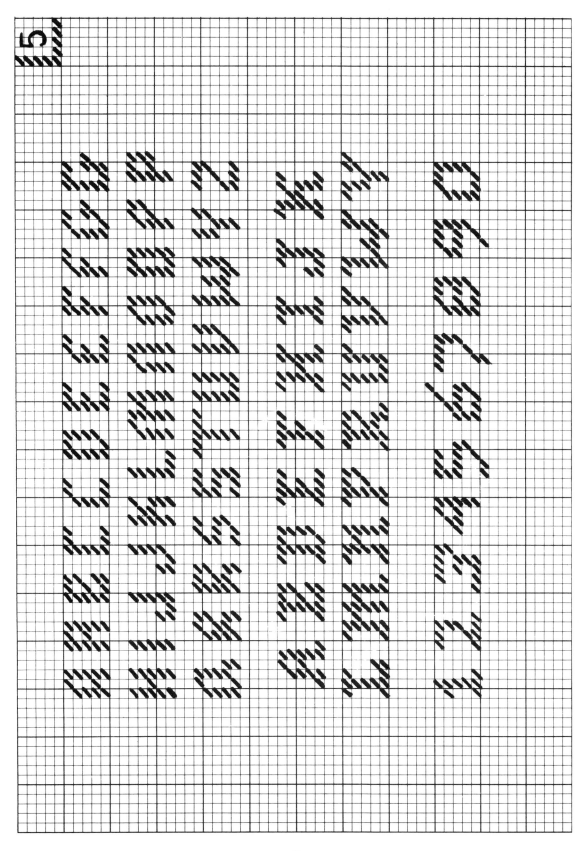

9

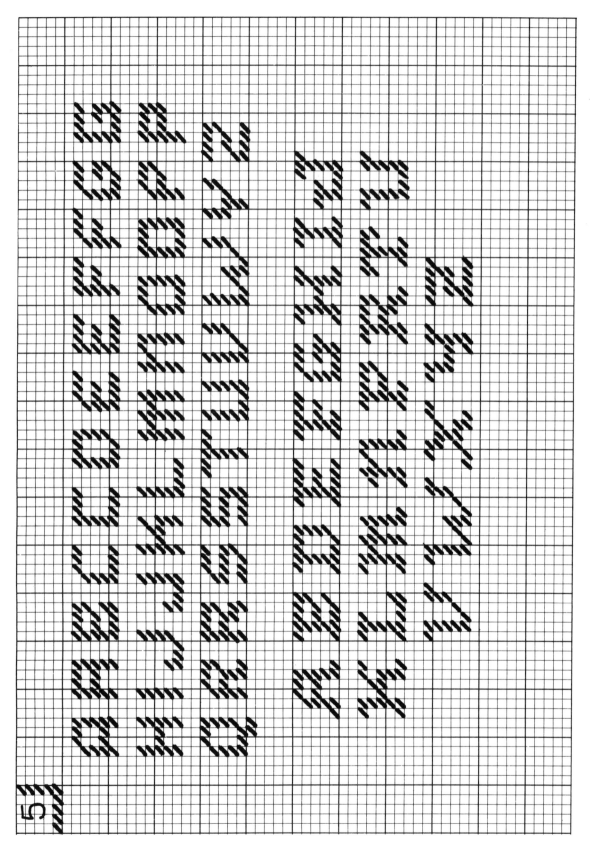

10

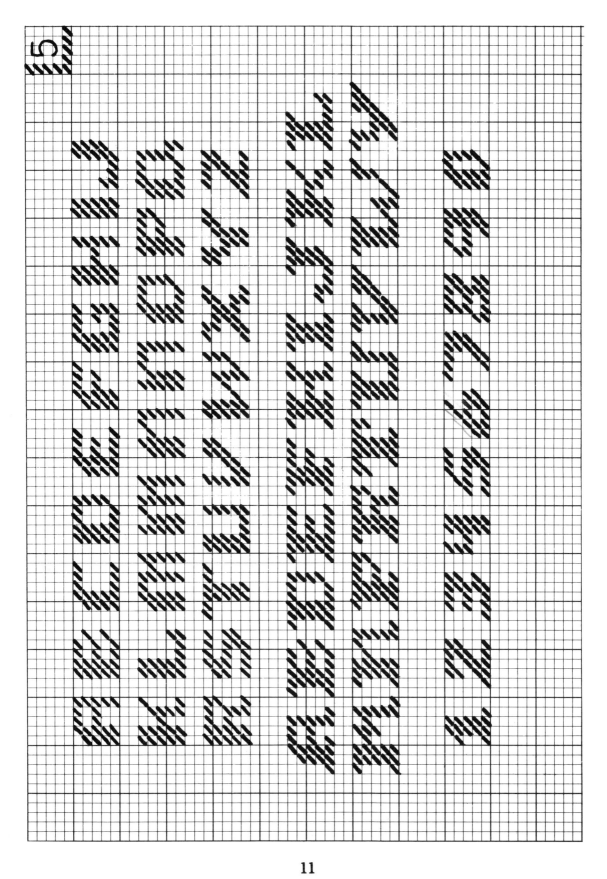

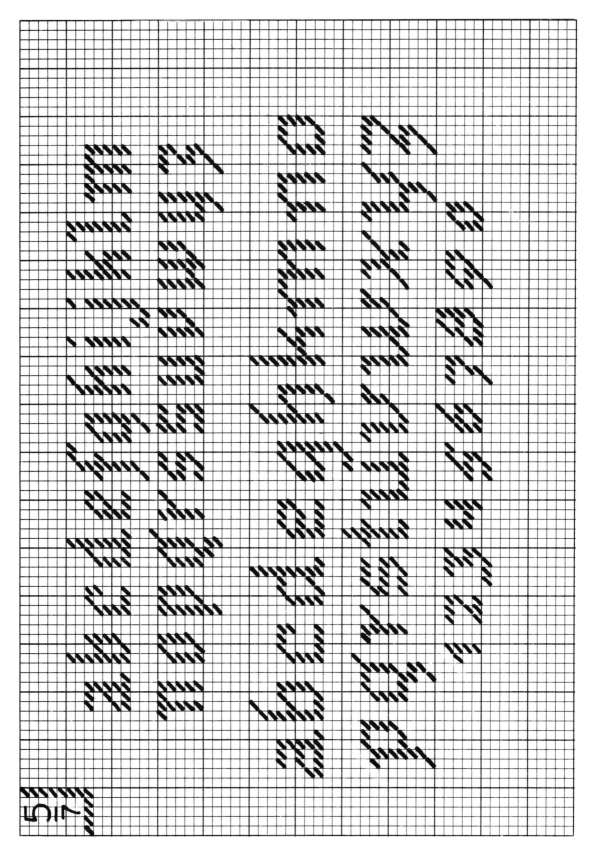

12

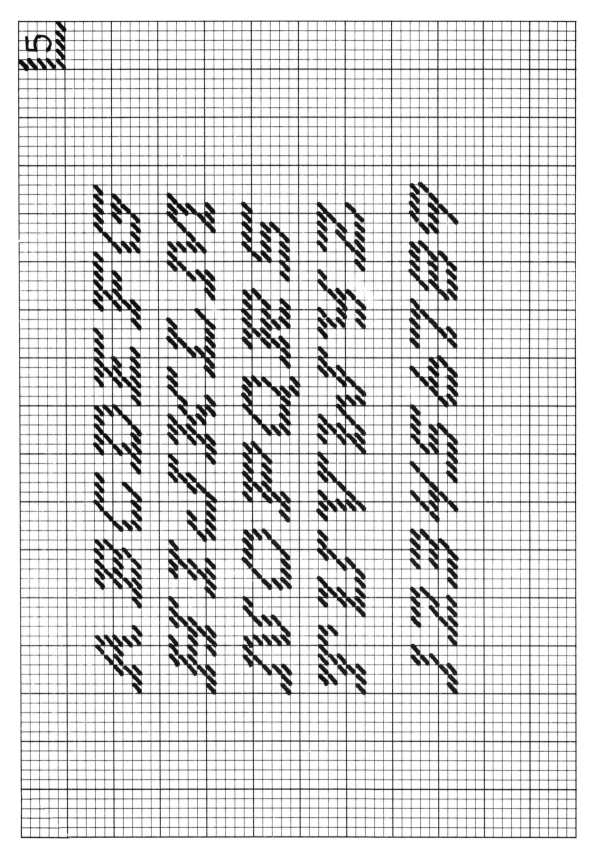

13

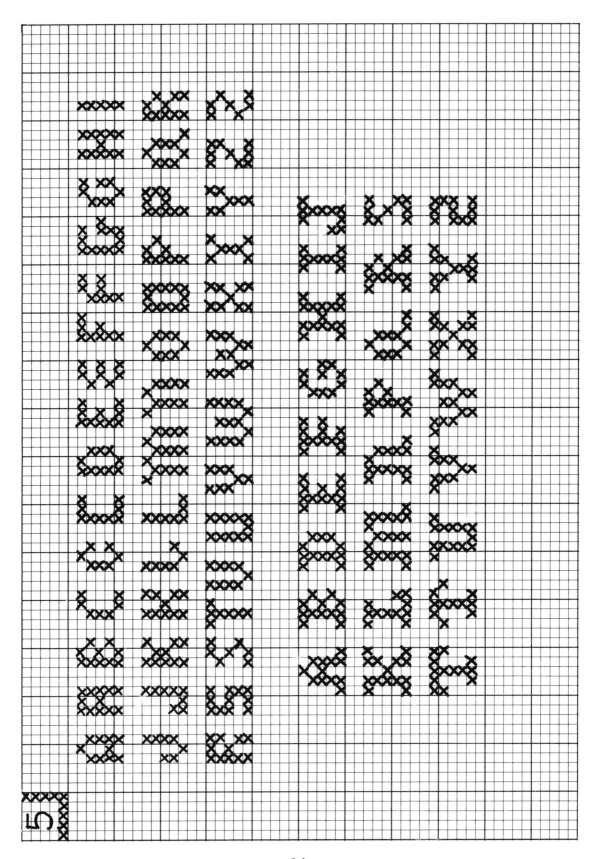

14

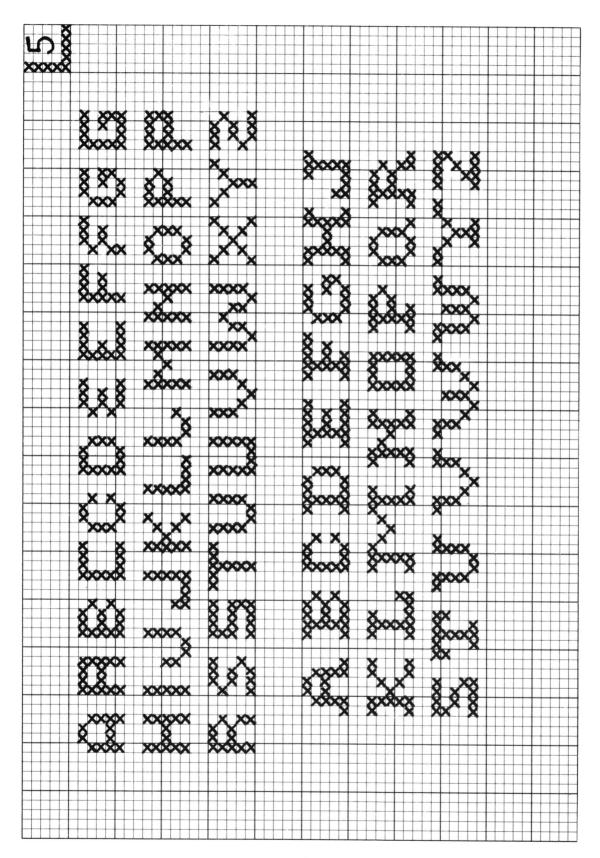

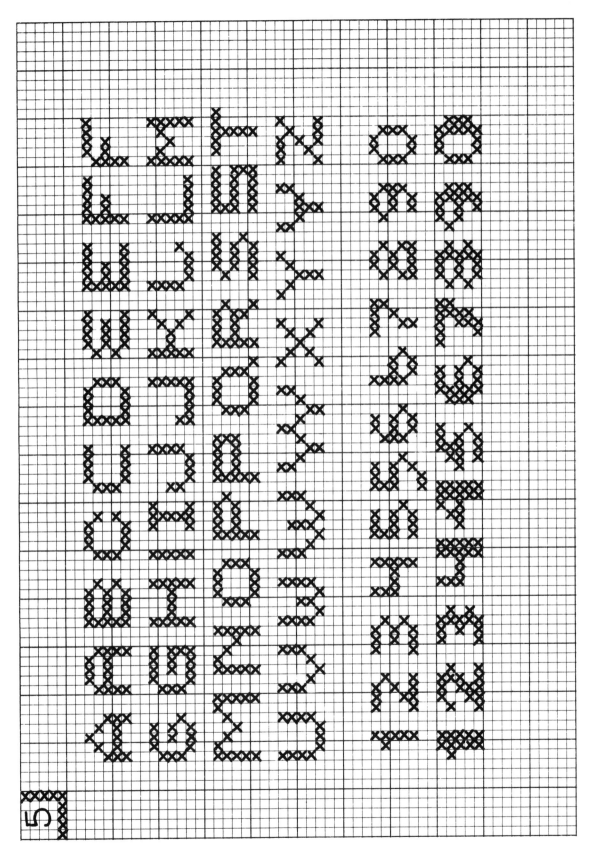

5

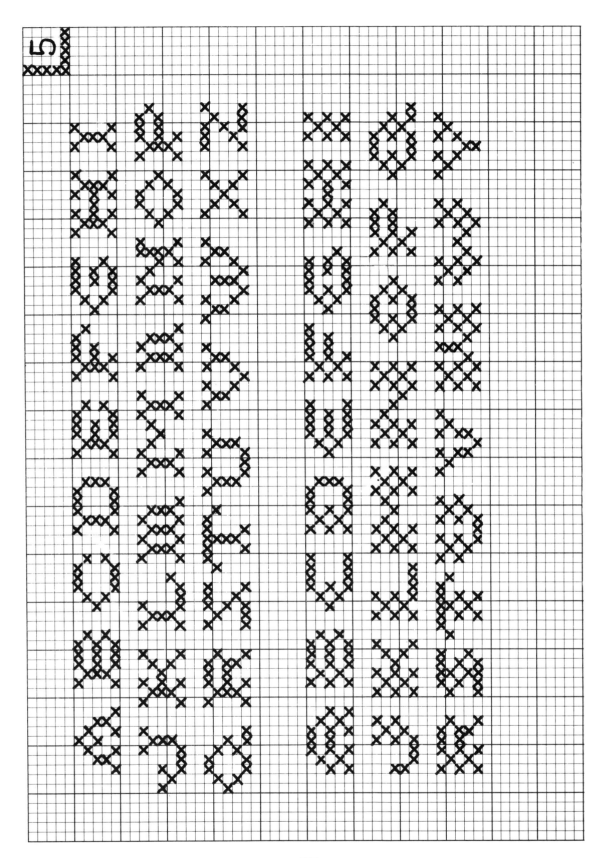

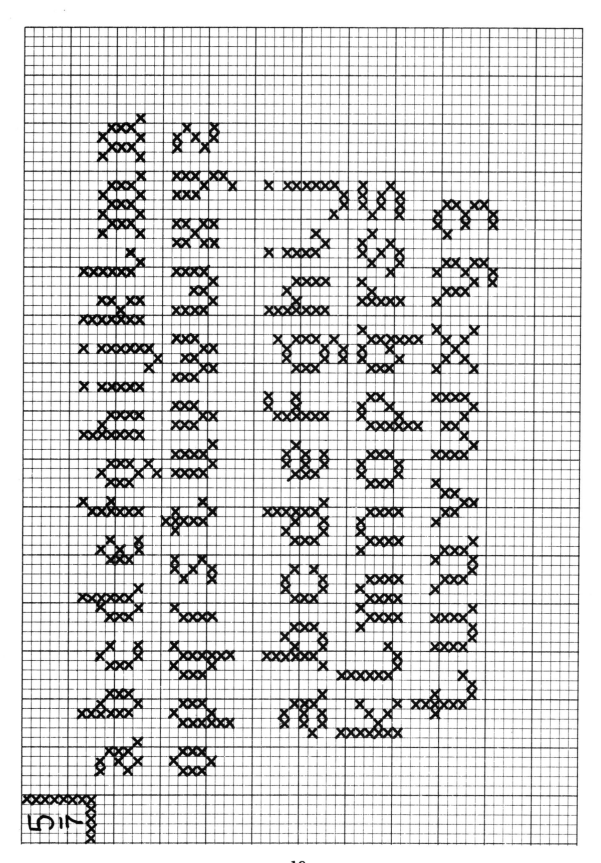

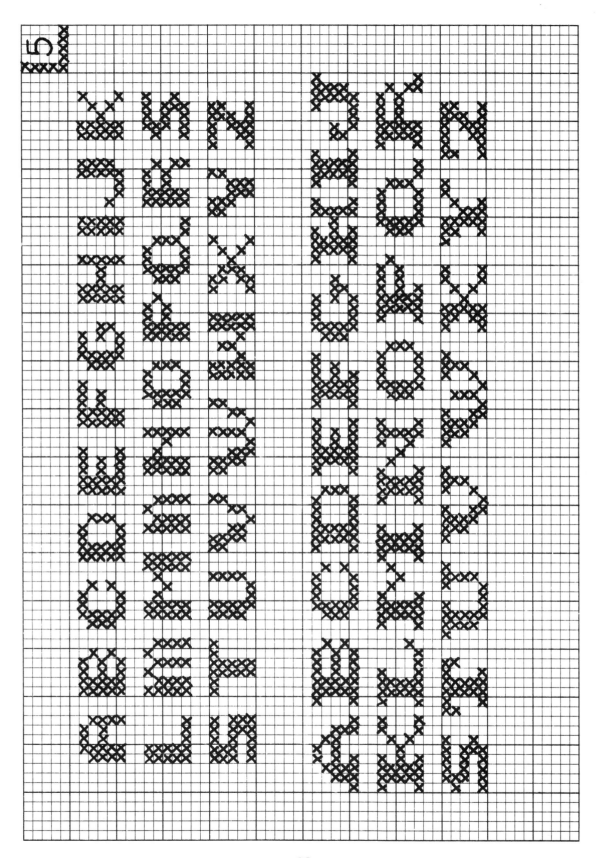

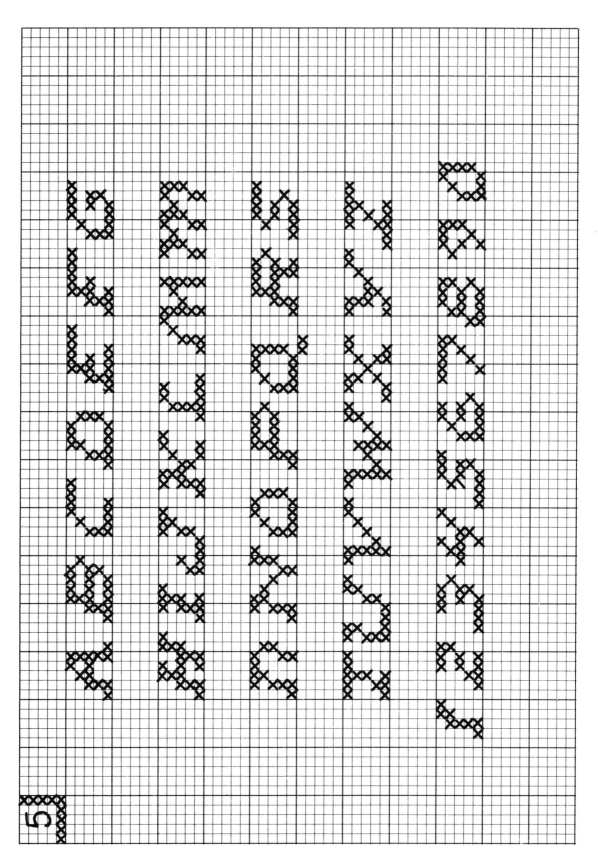

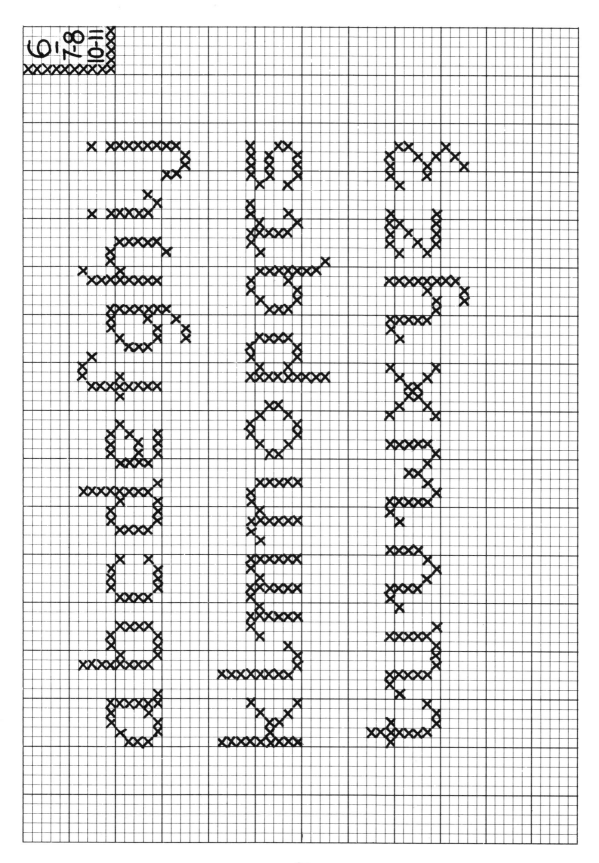

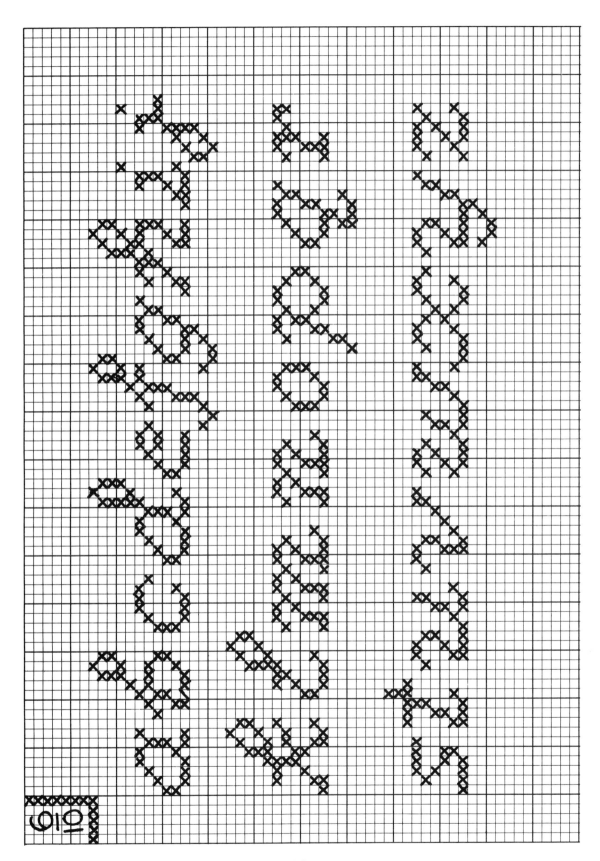

22

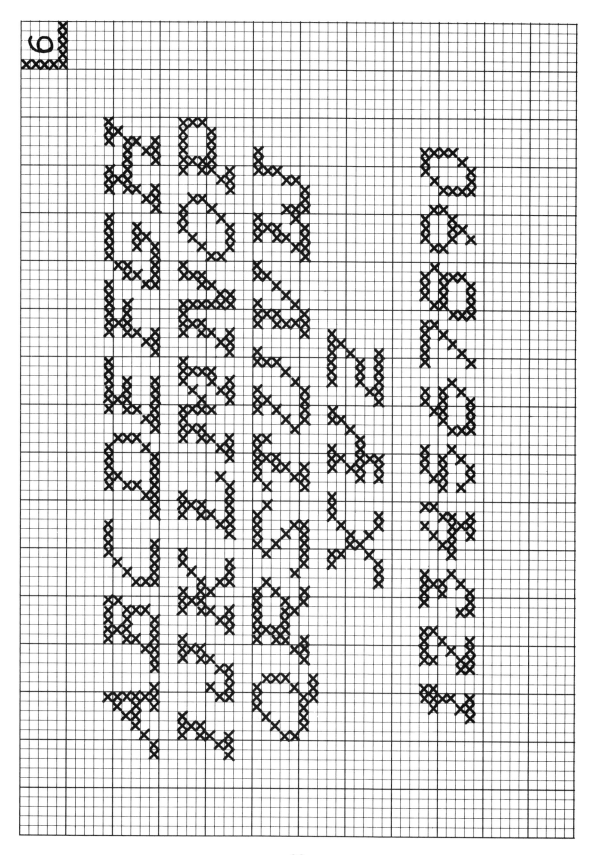

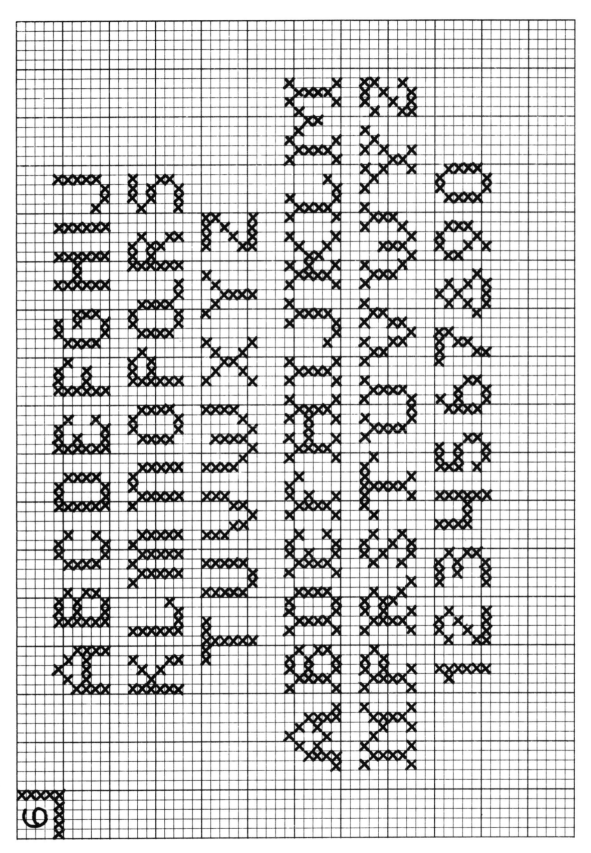

24

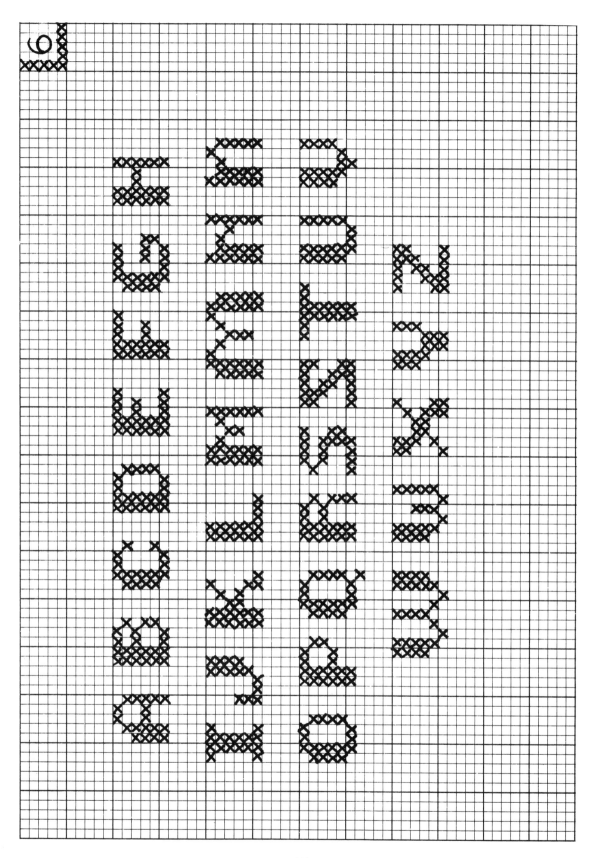

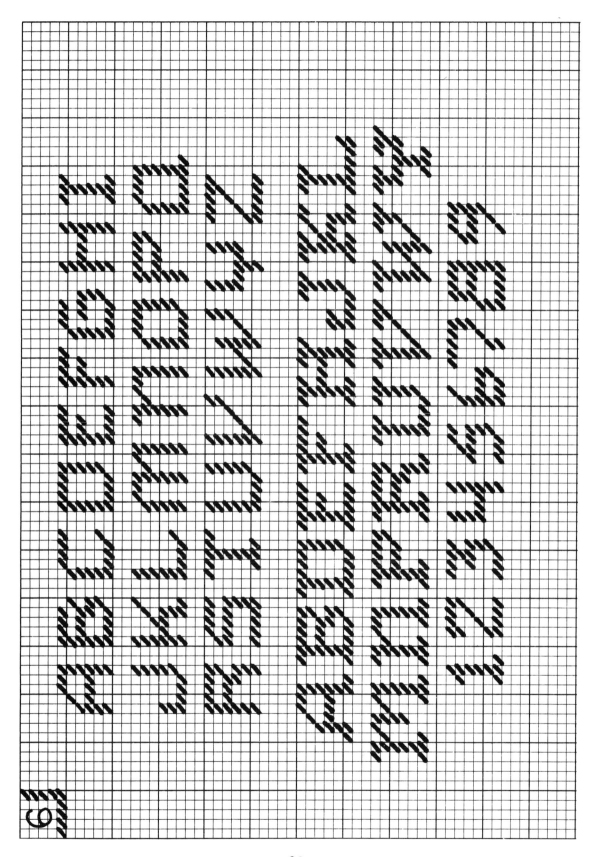

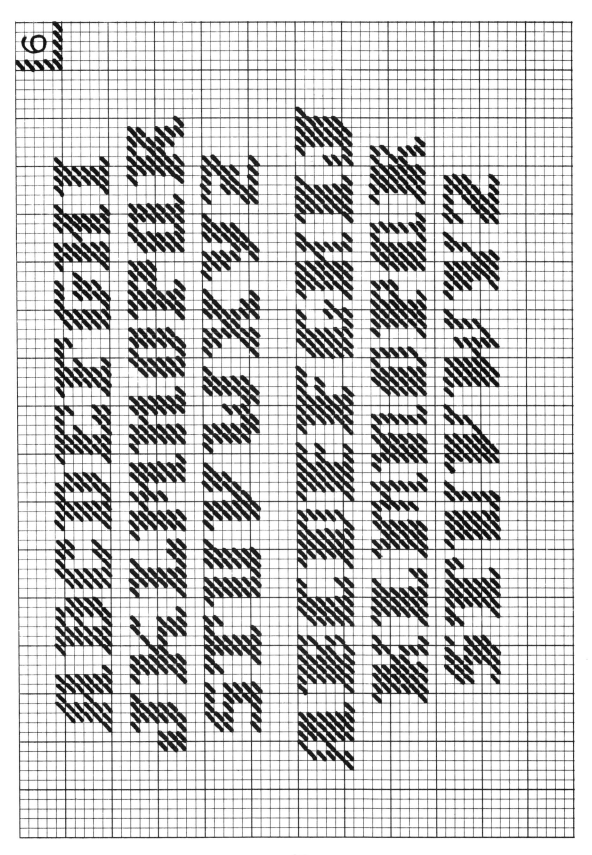

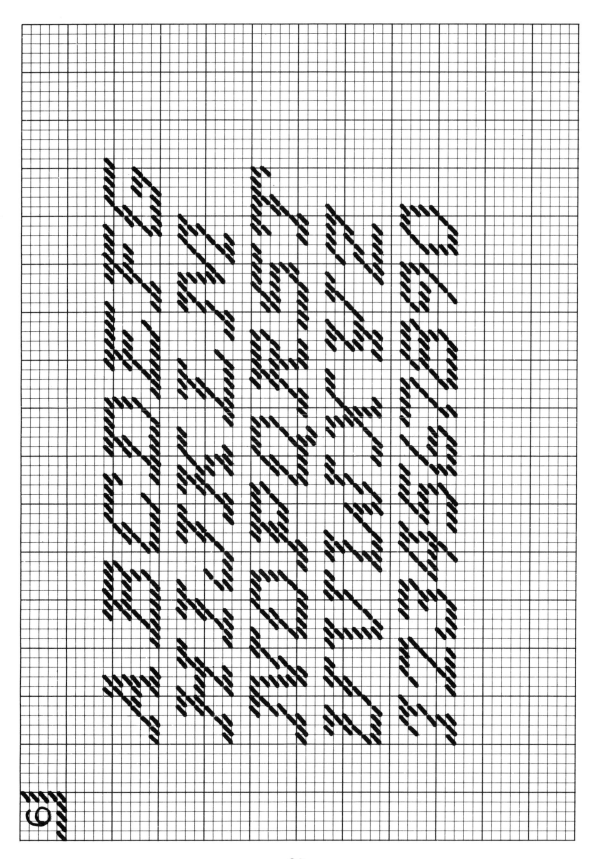

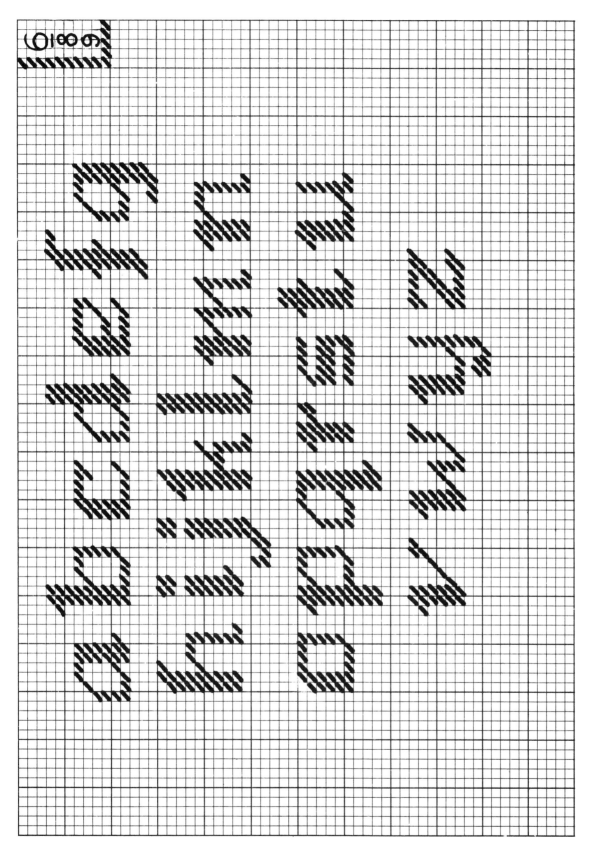

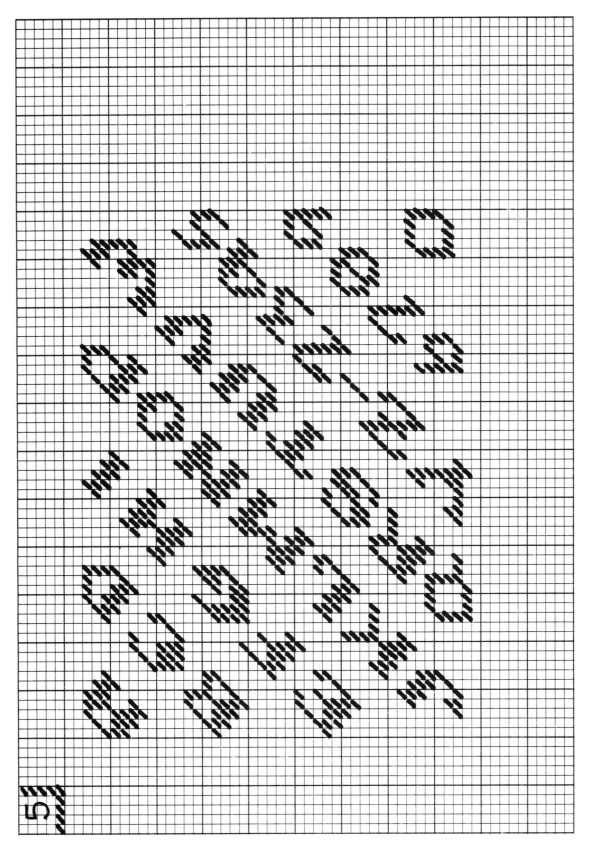

51

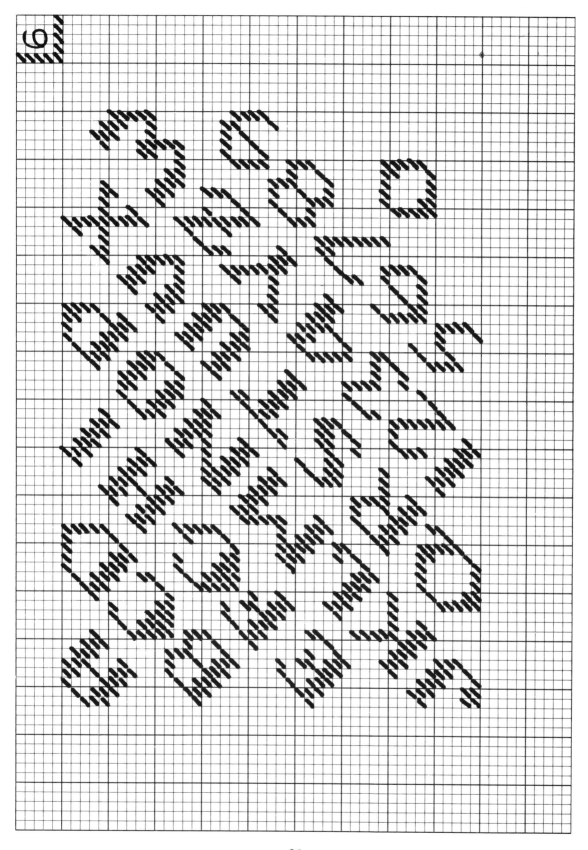

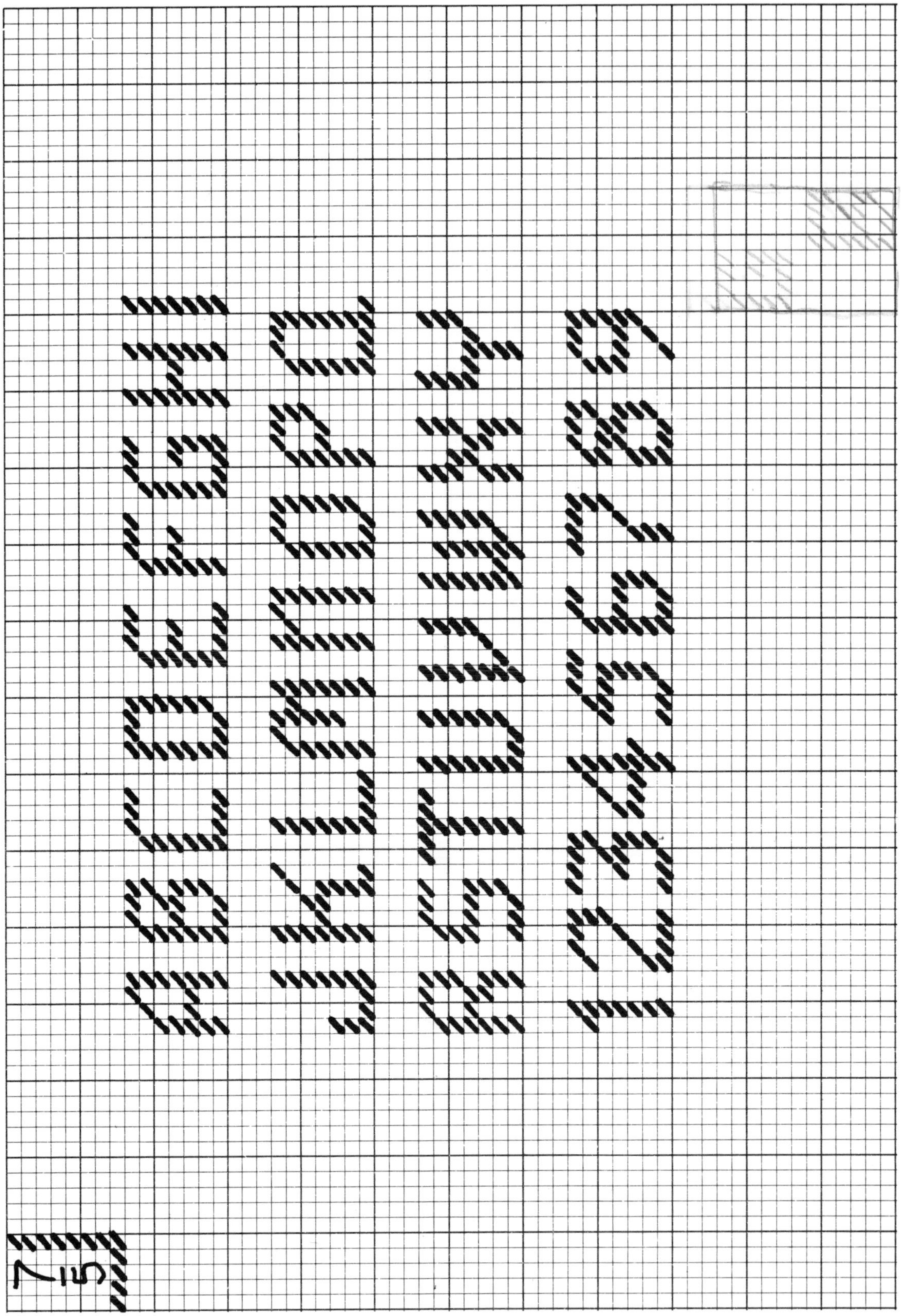

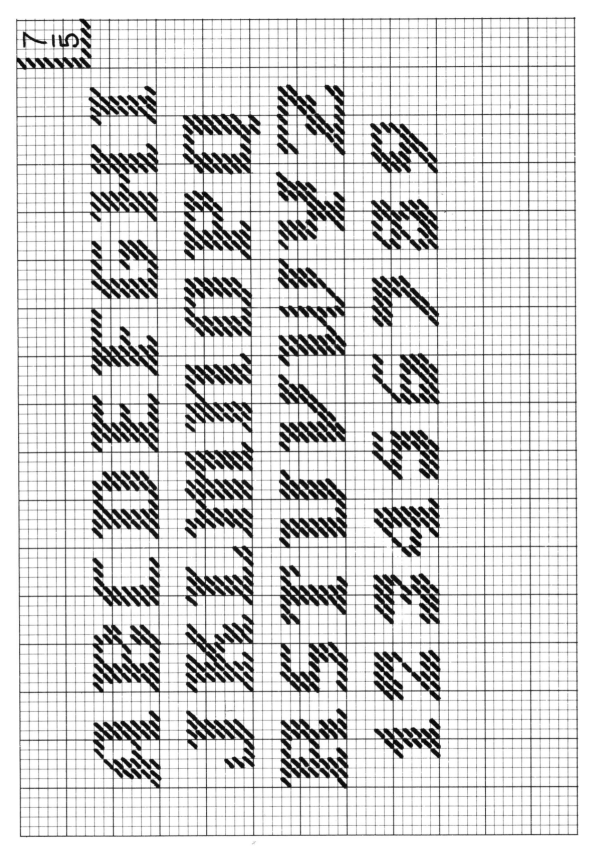

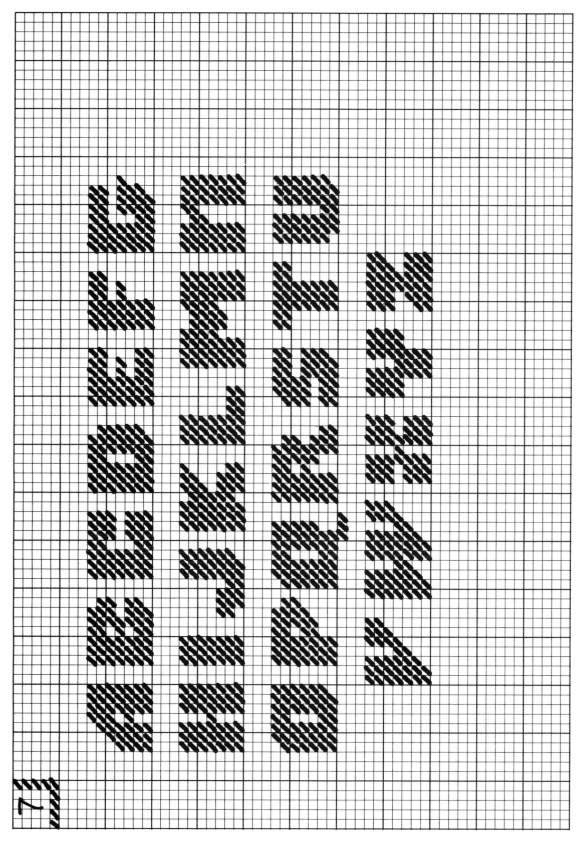

34

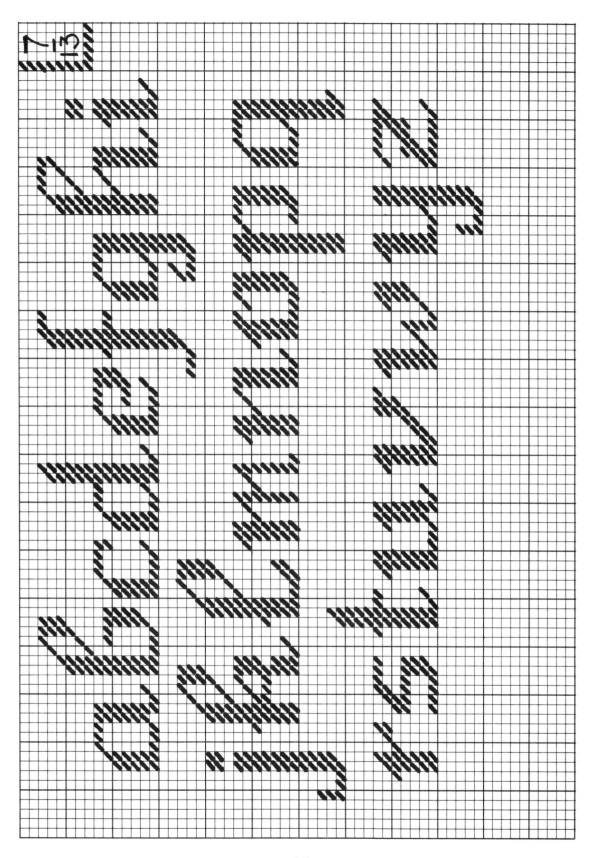

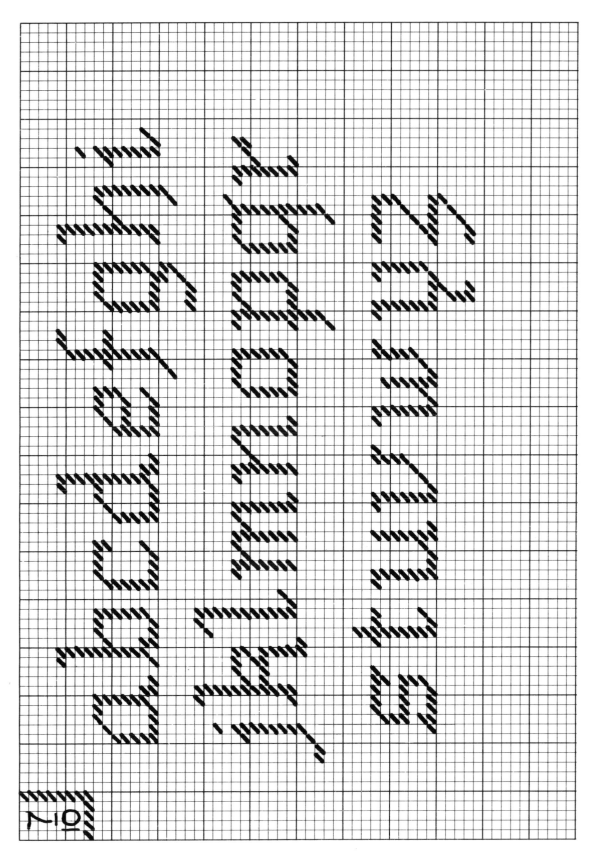

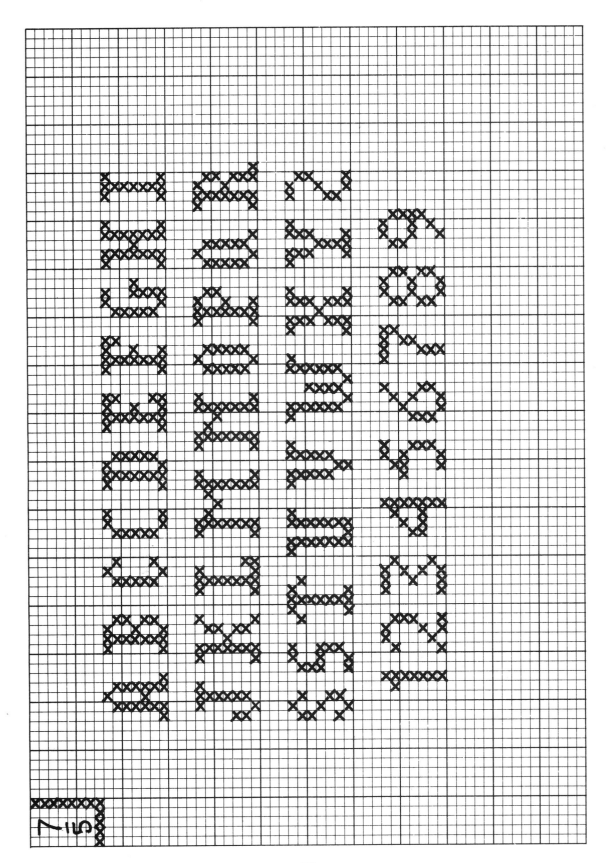

38

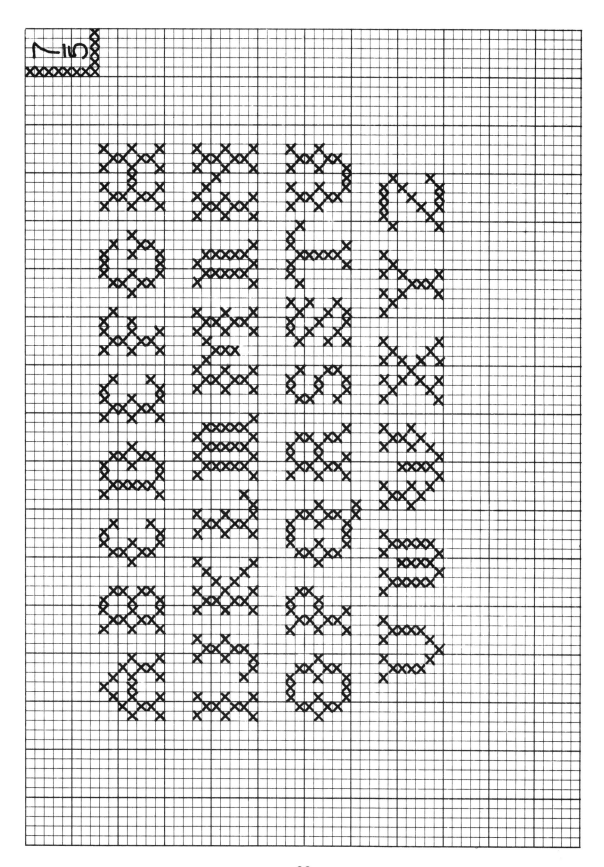

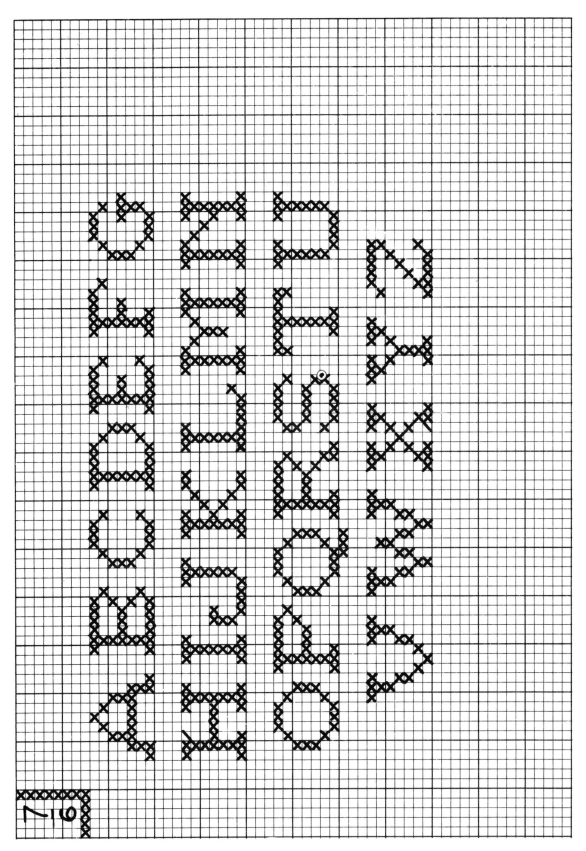

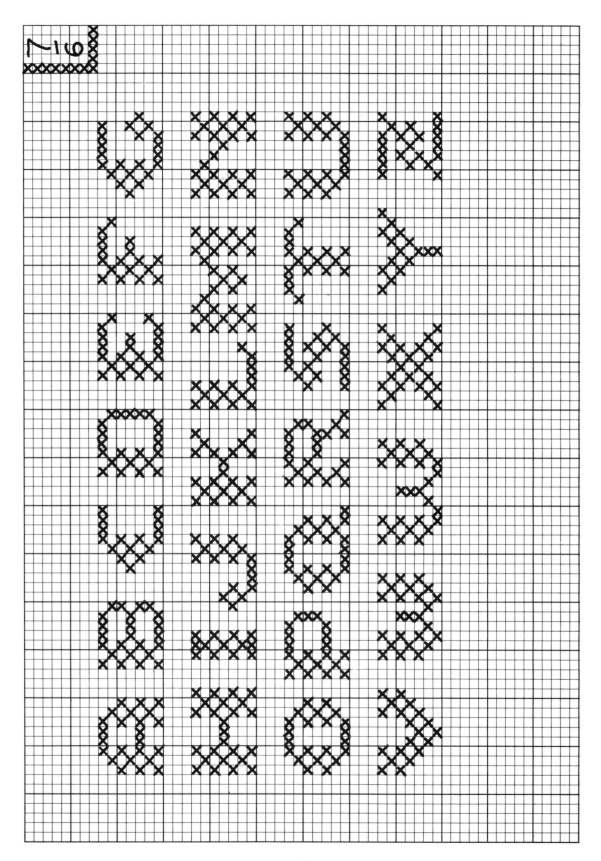

41

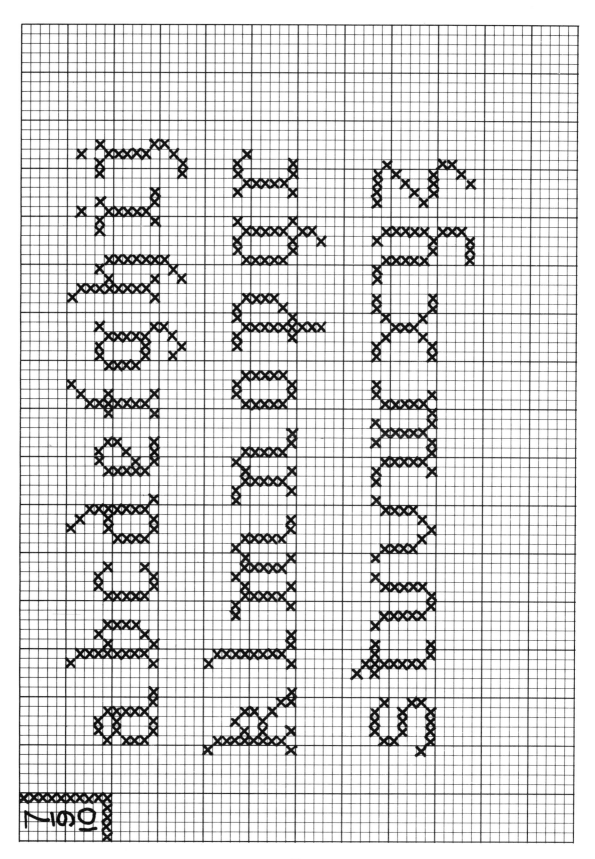

42

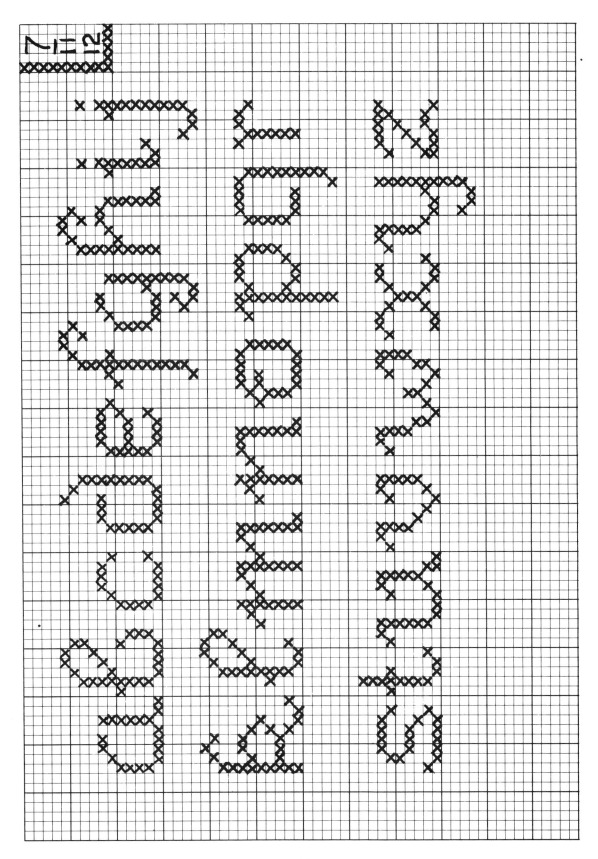

43

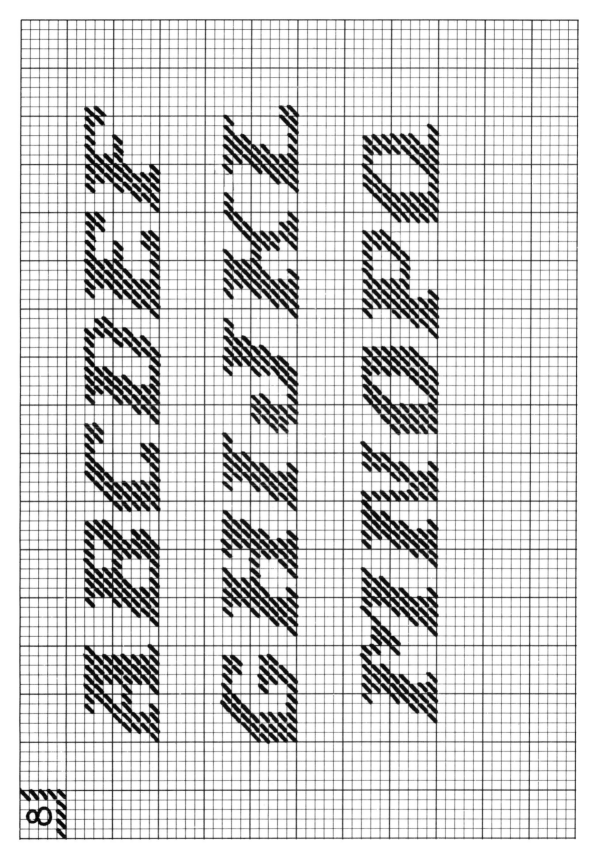

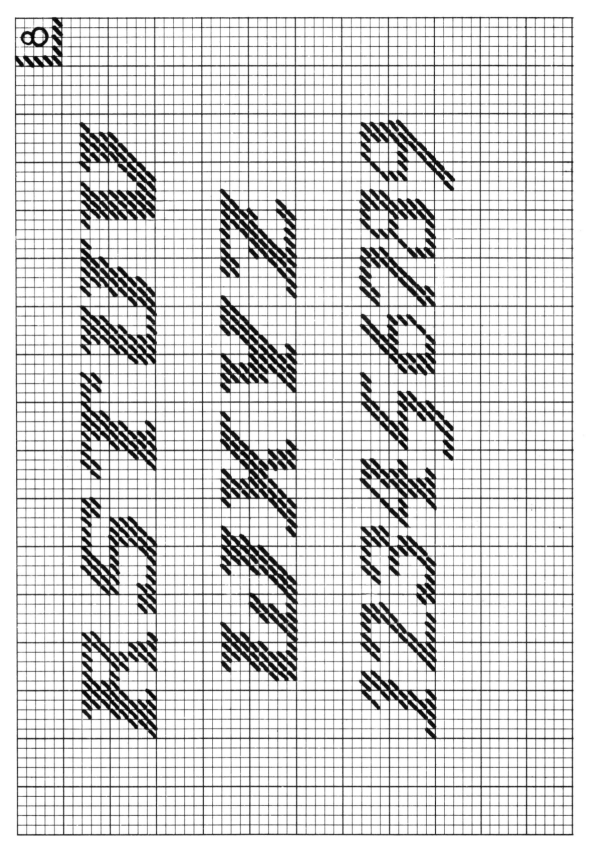

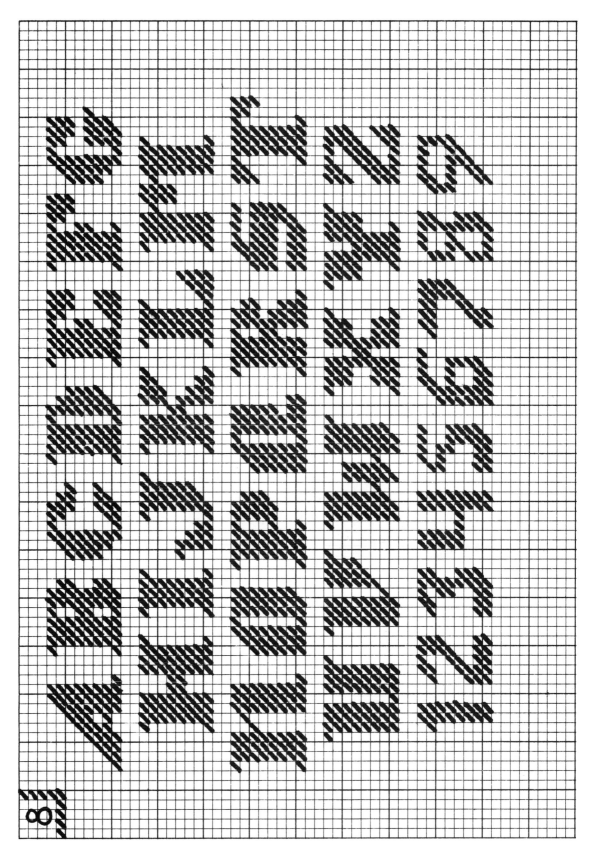

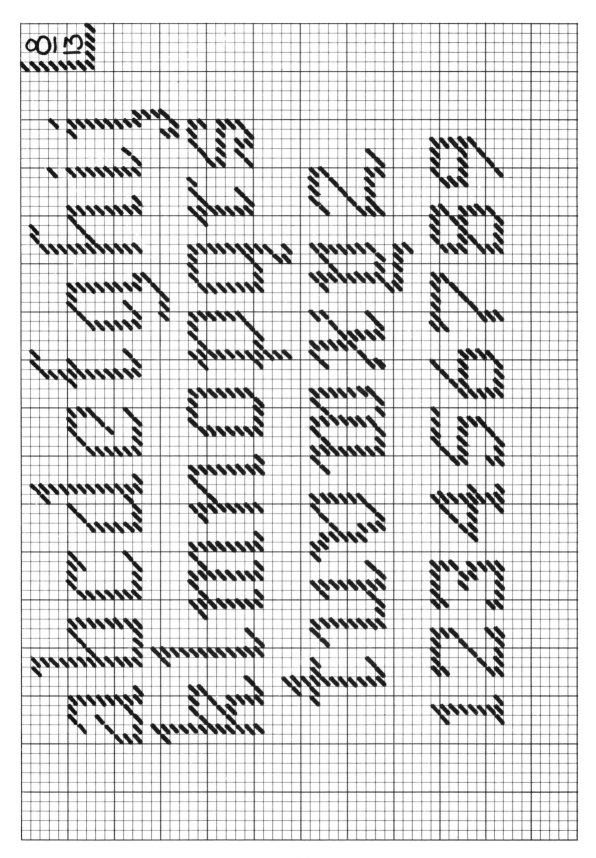

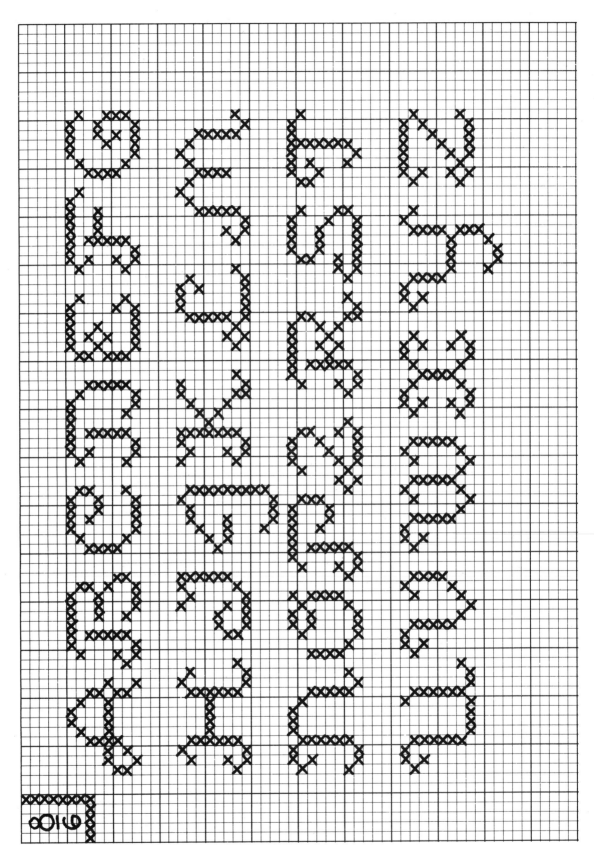

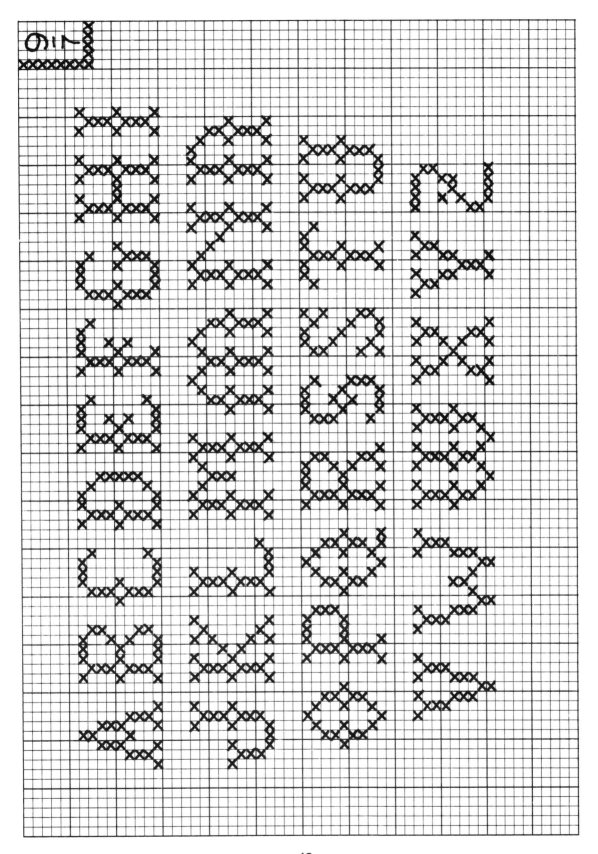

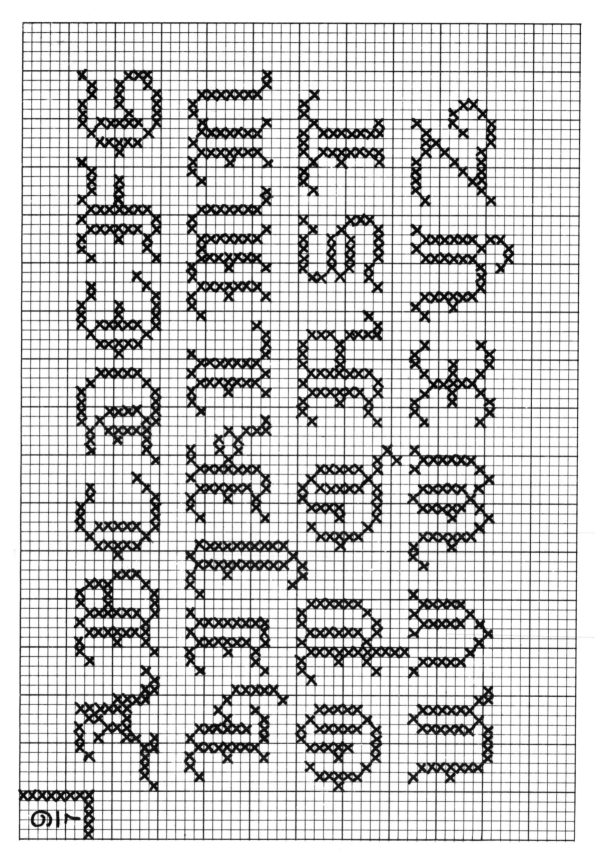

50

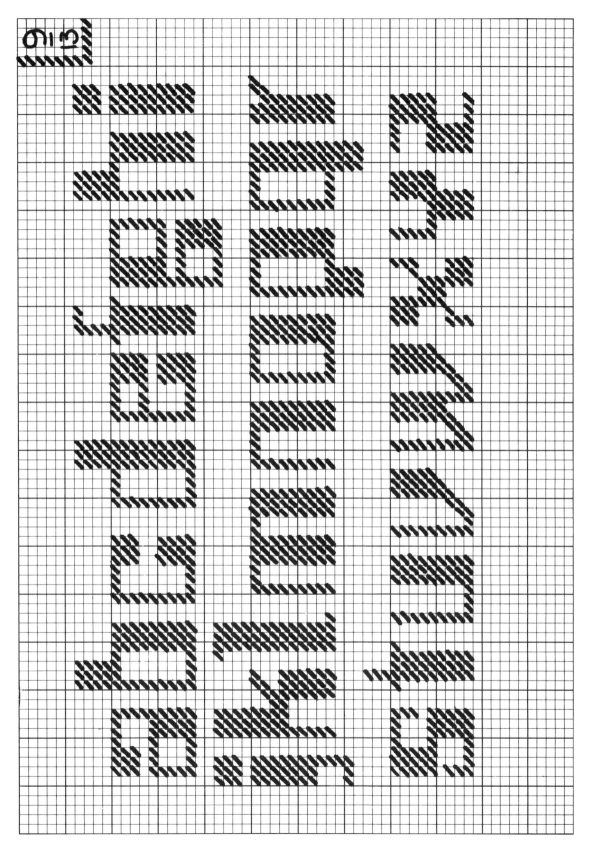

51

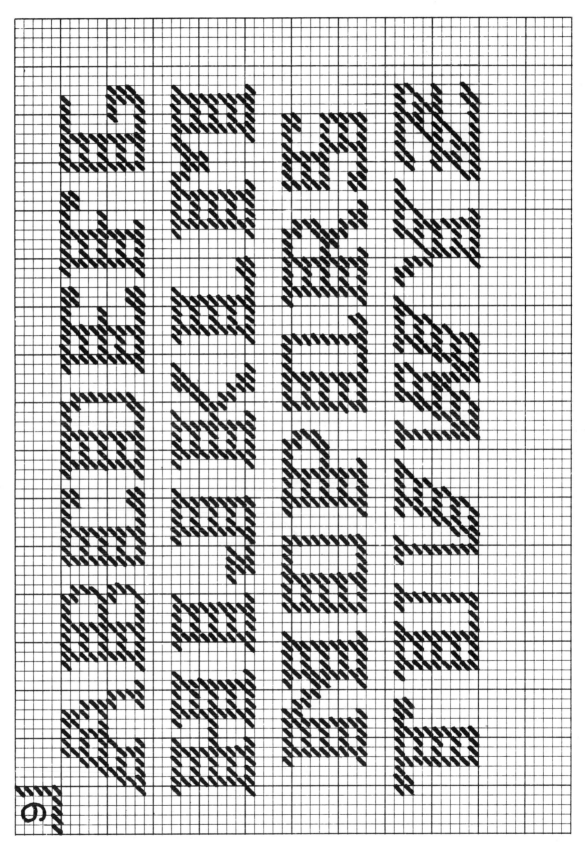

52

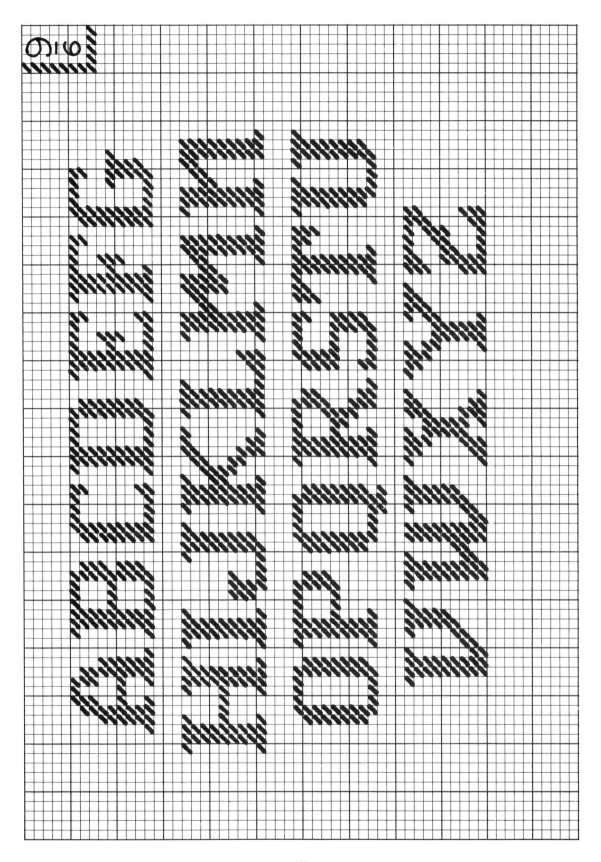

53

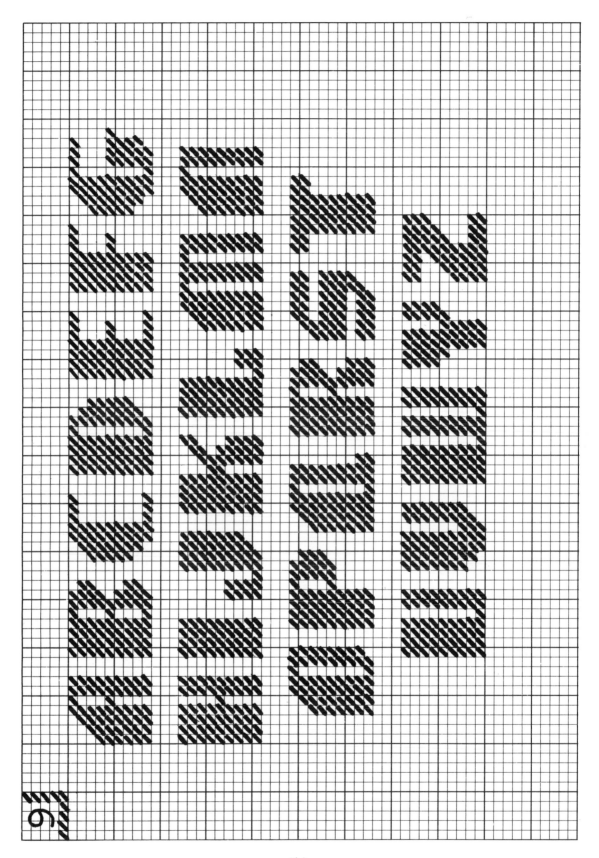

54

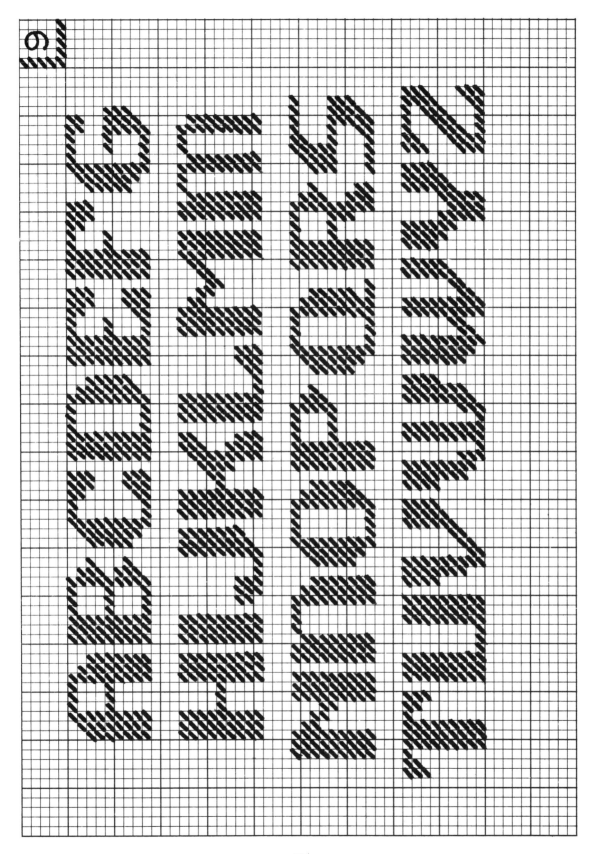

55

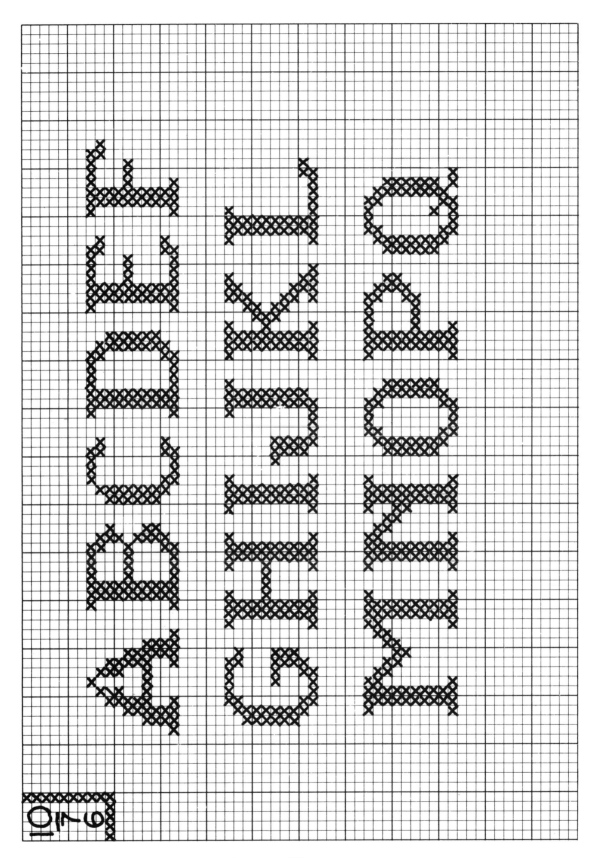

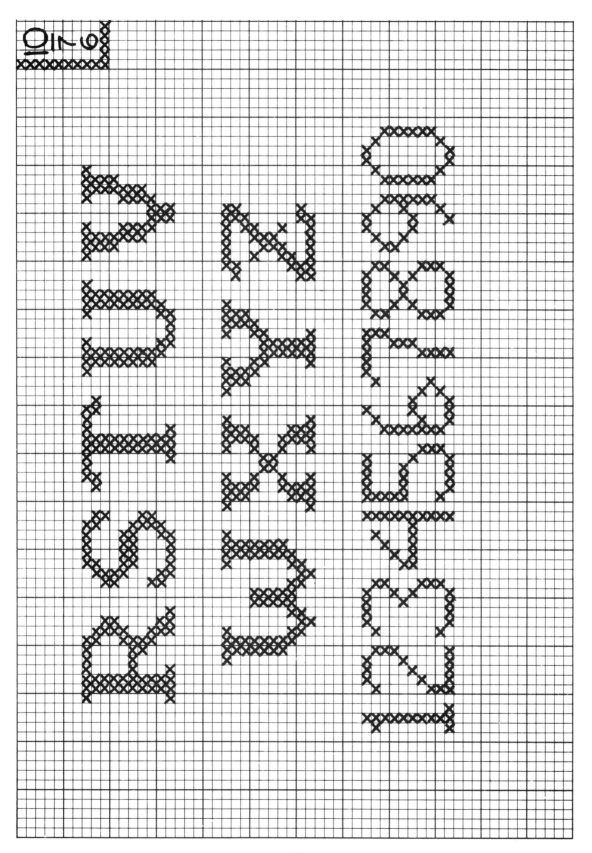

57

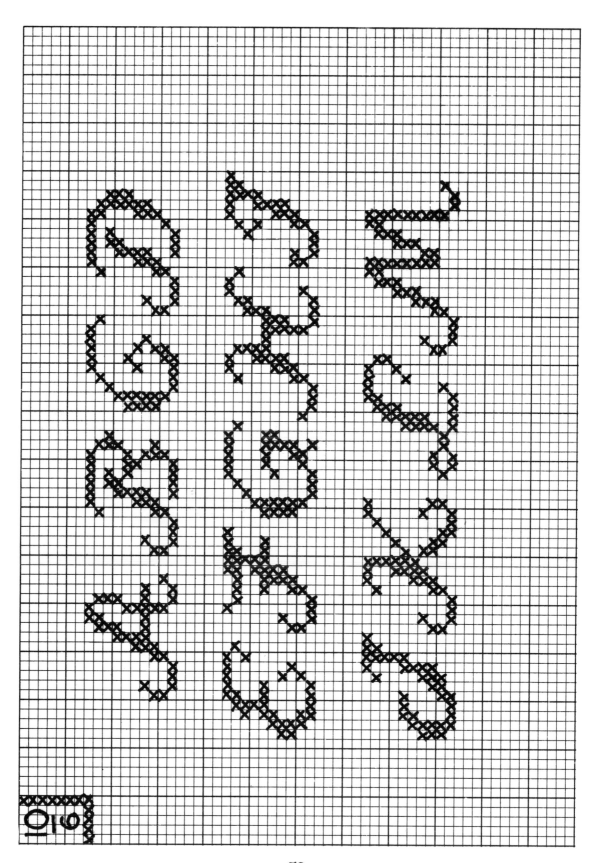

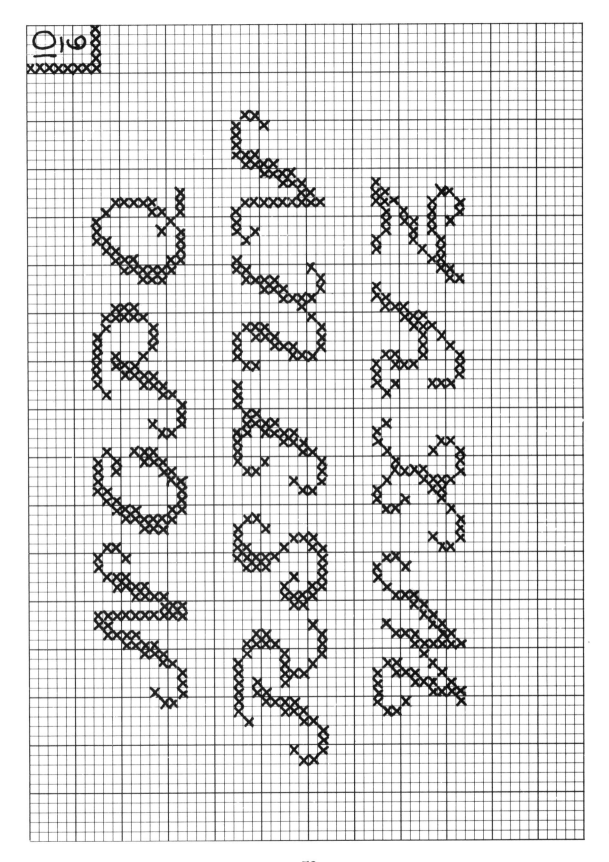

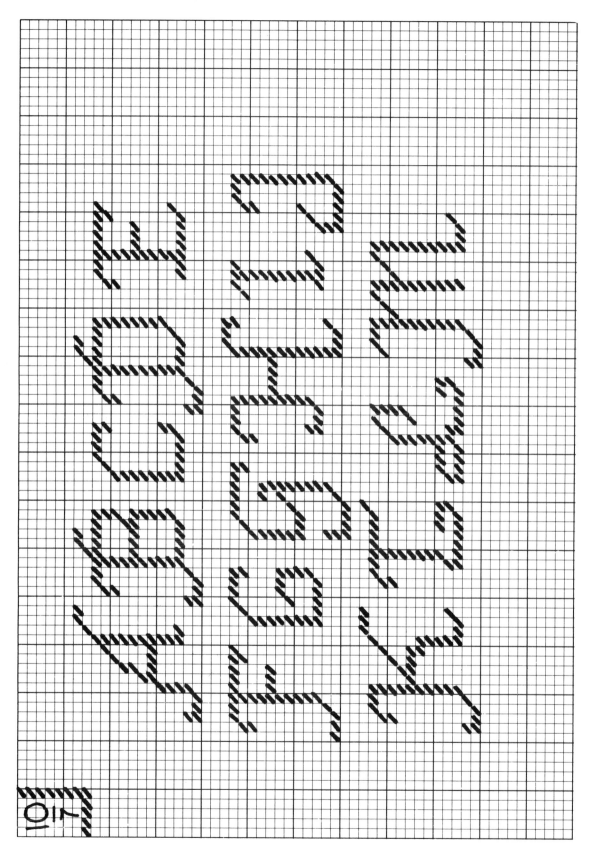

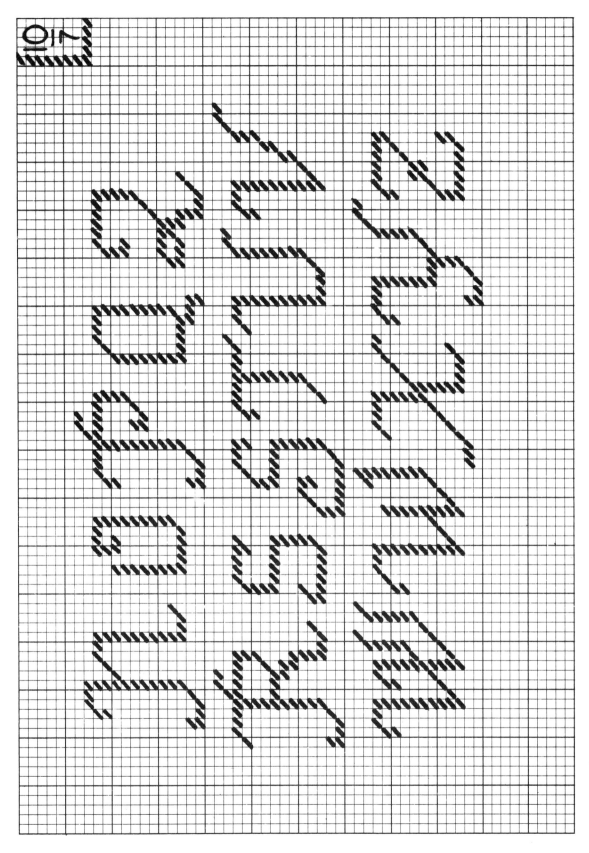

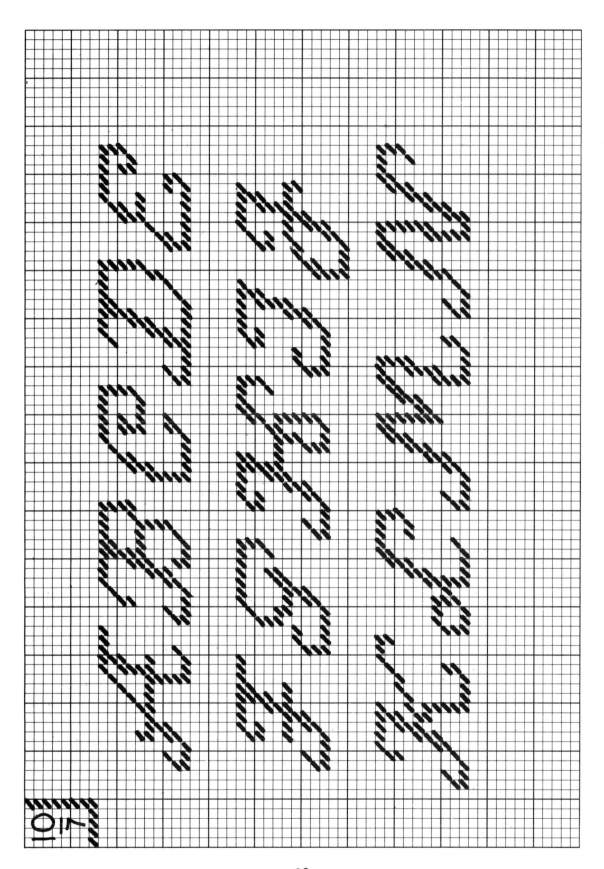

62

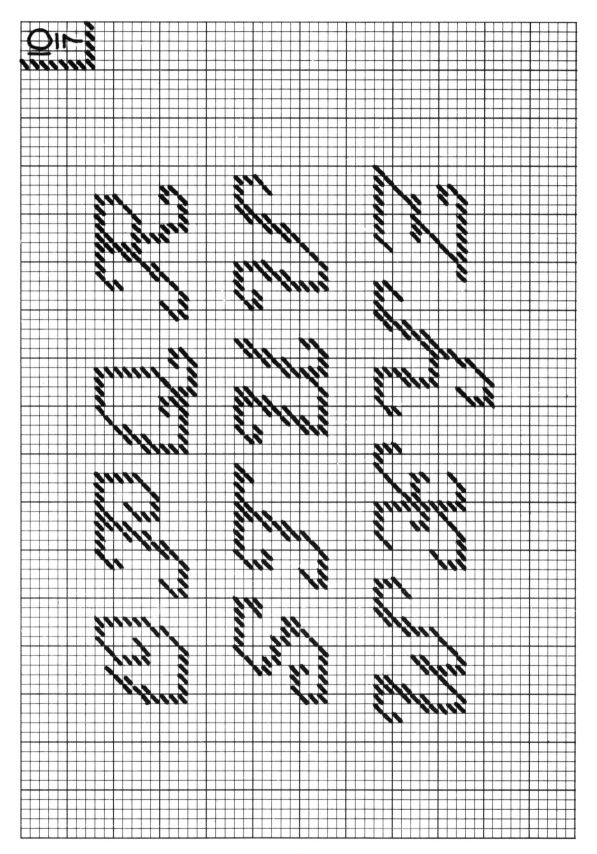

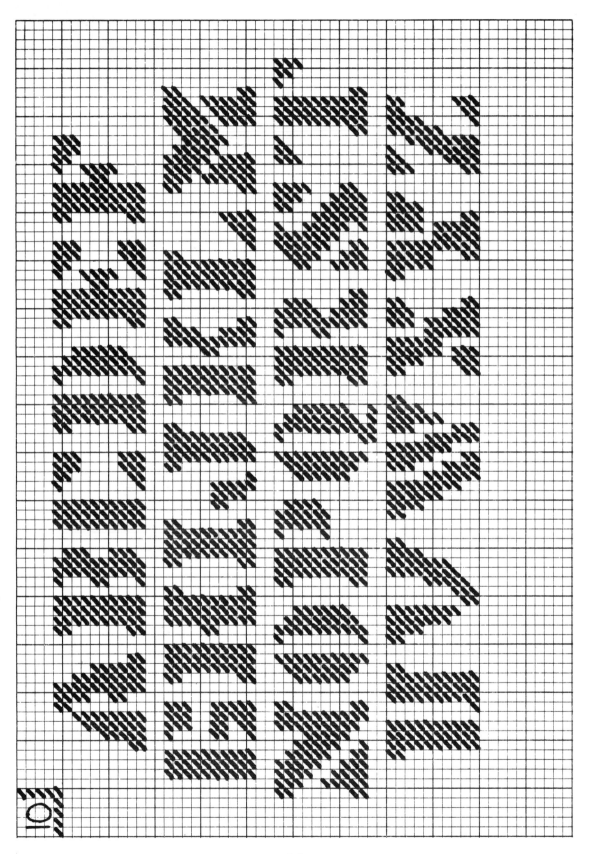

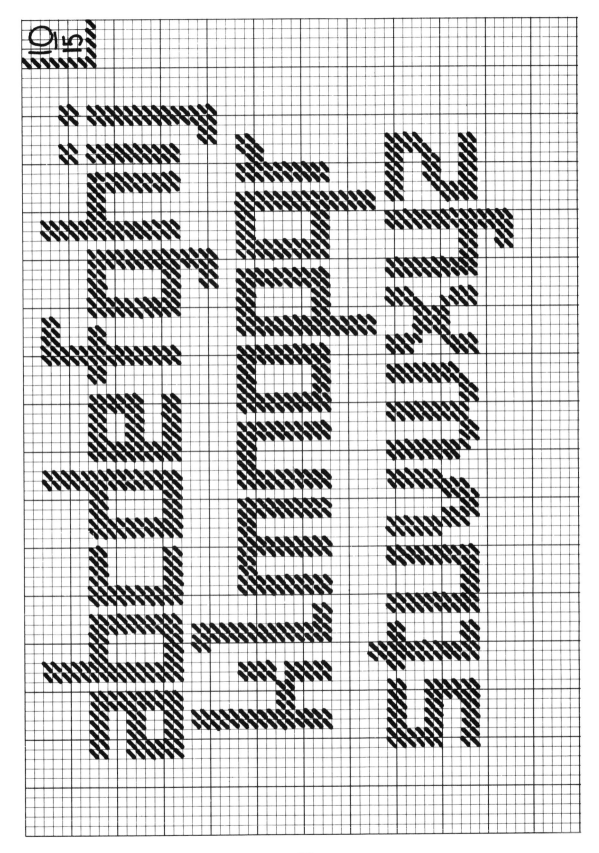

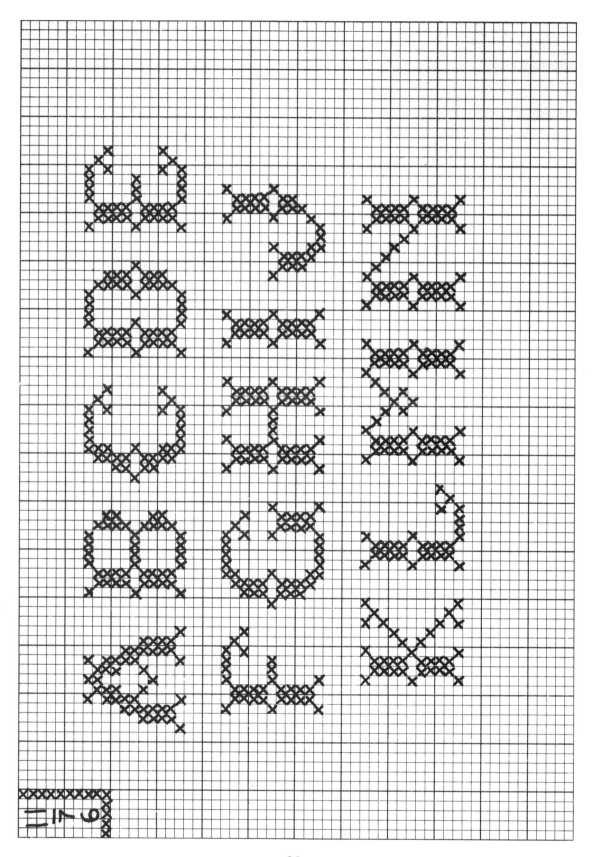

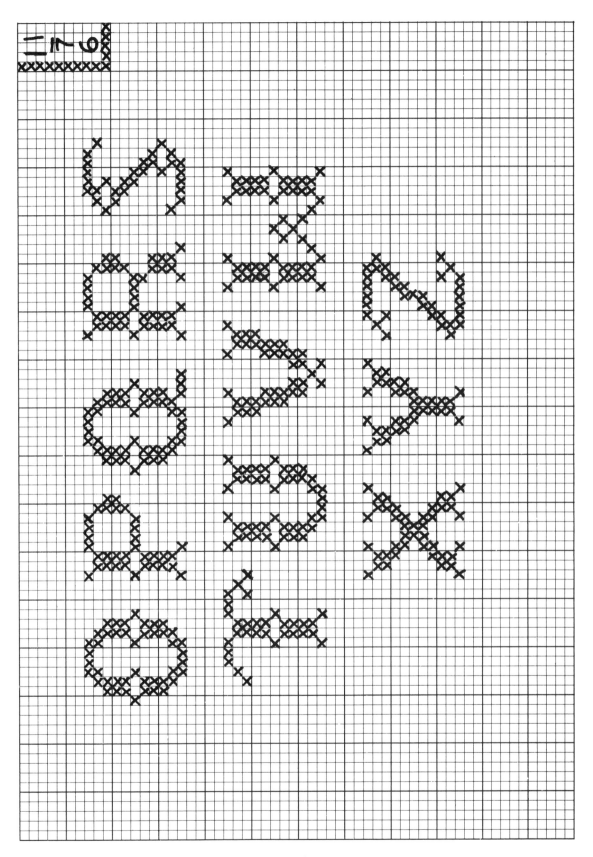

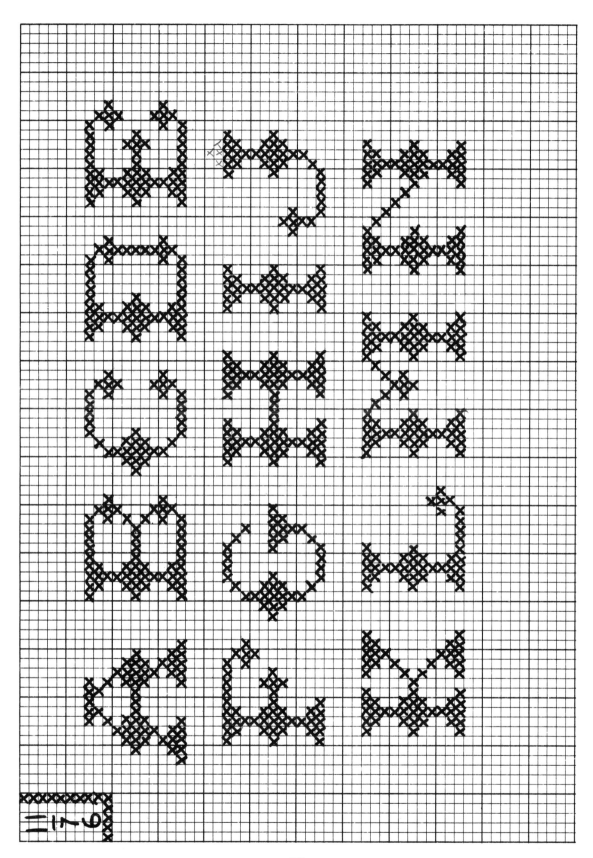

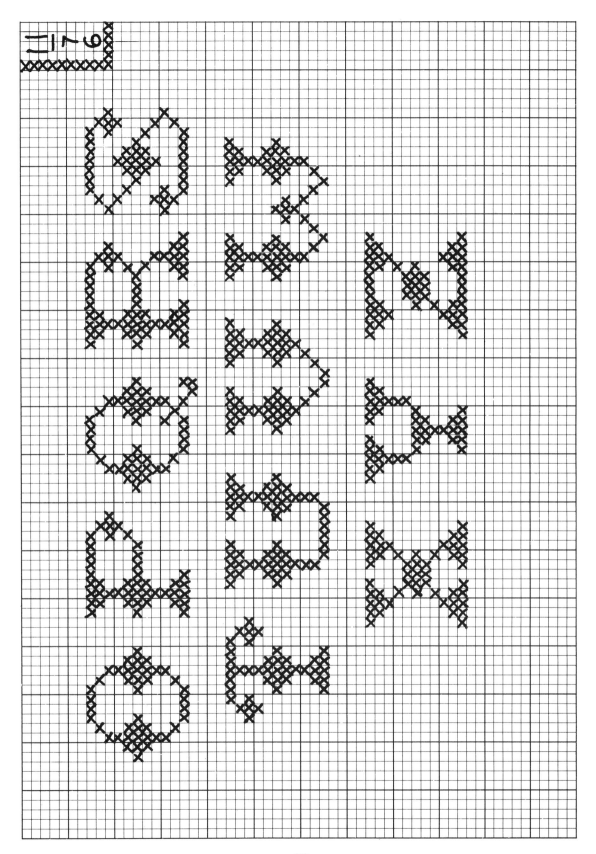

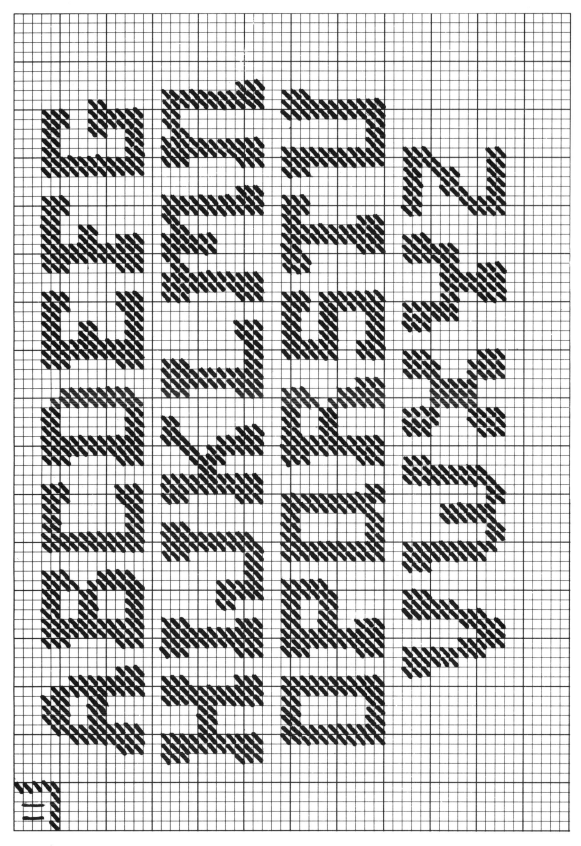

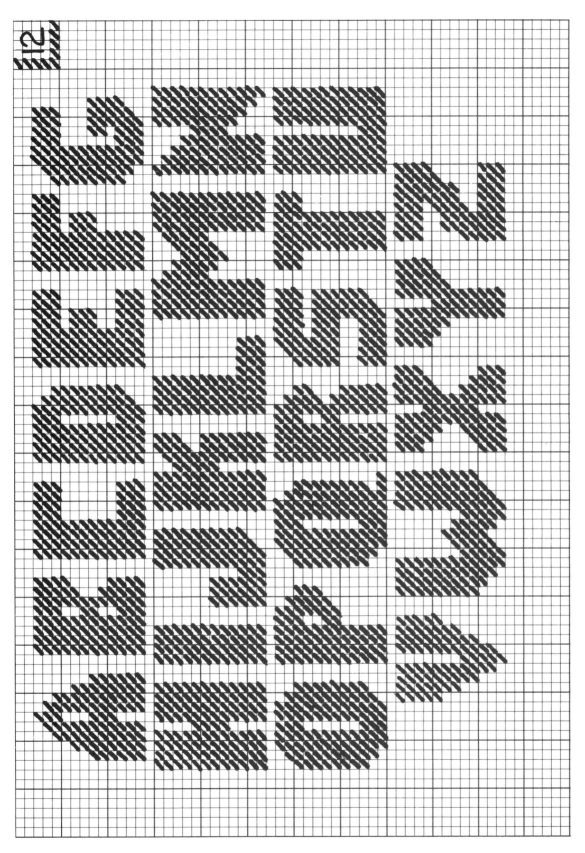

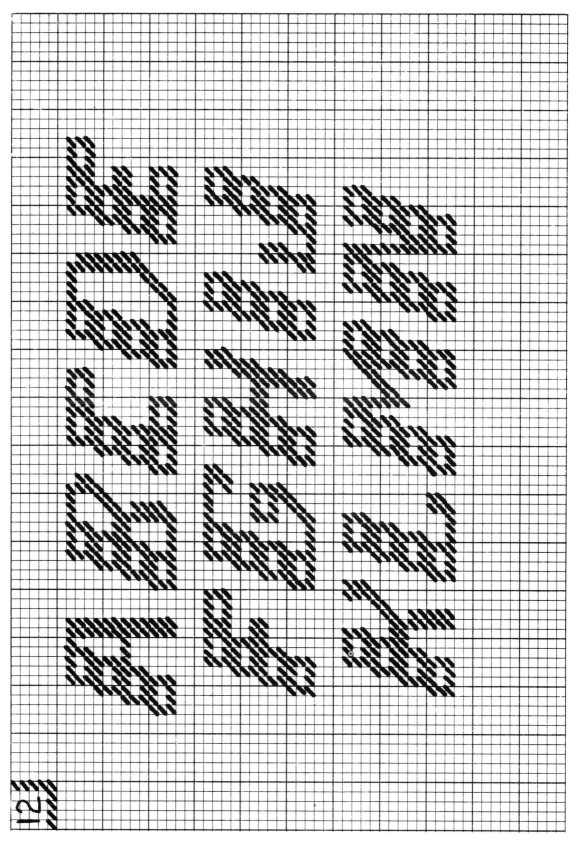

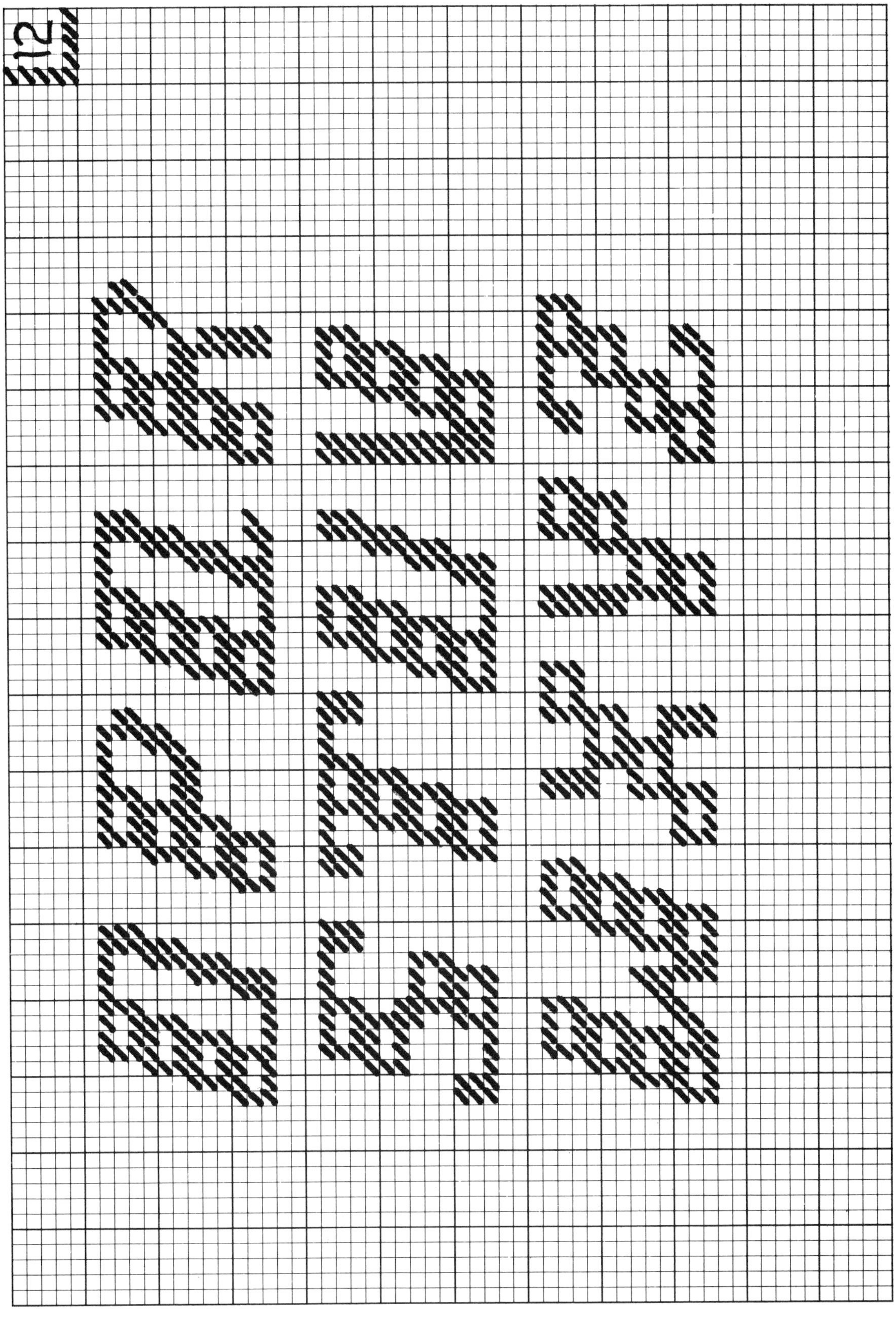
12

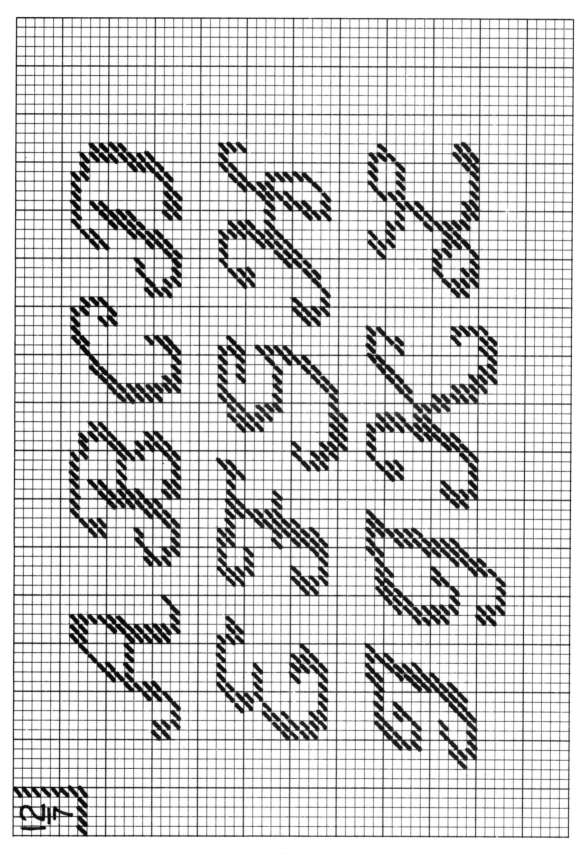

74

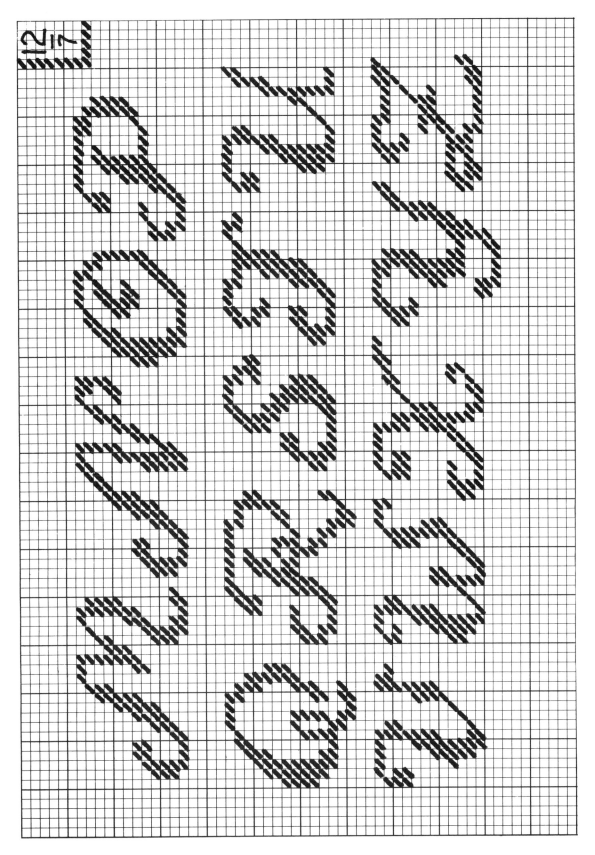

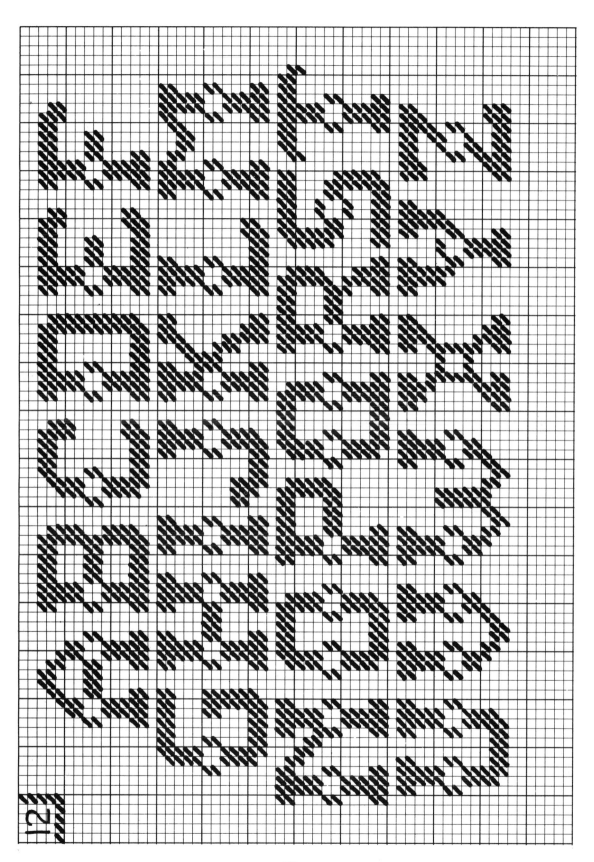

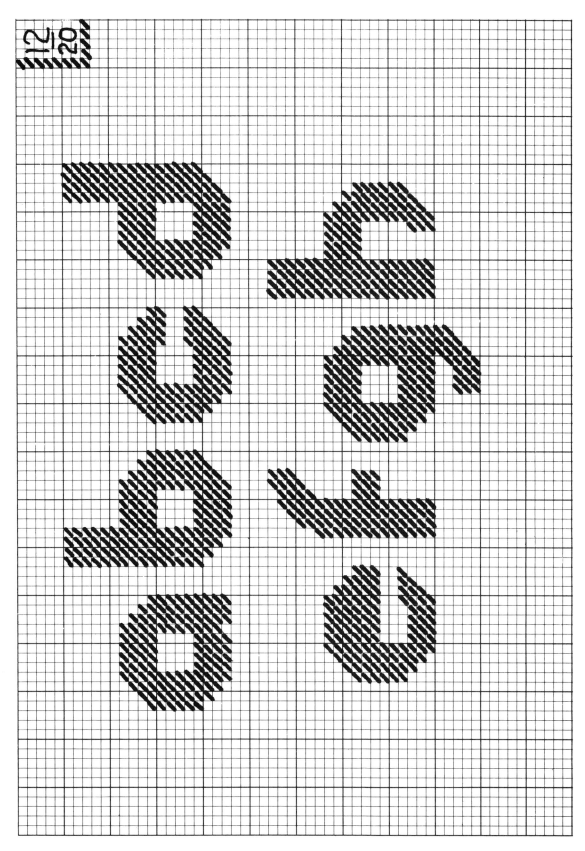

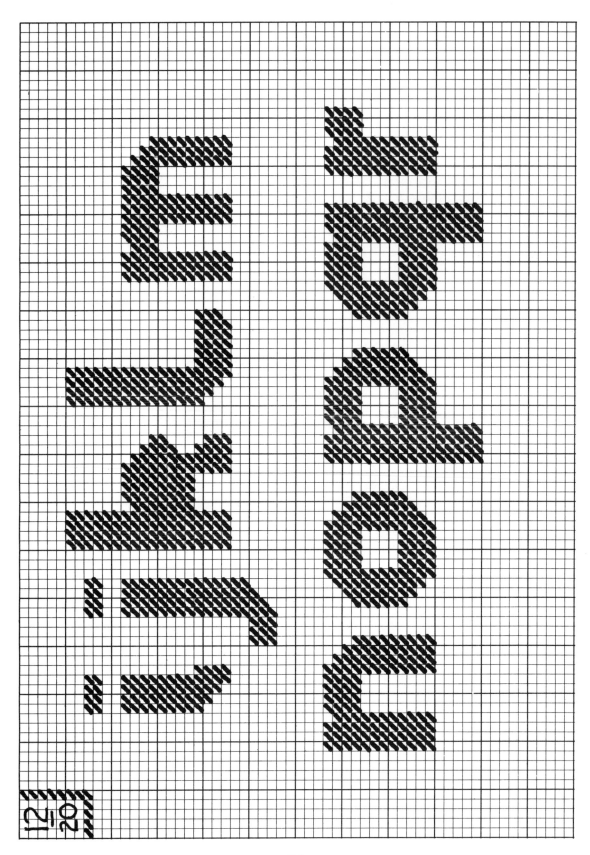

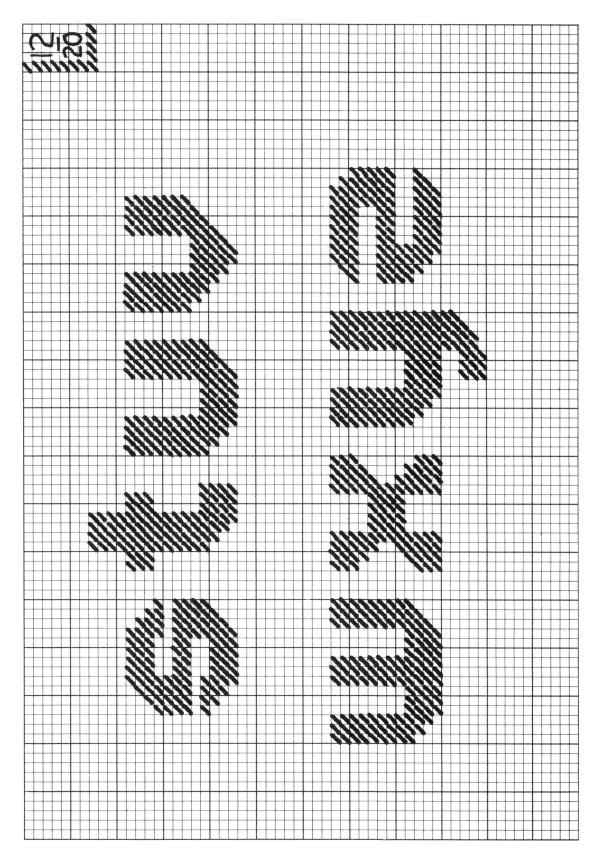

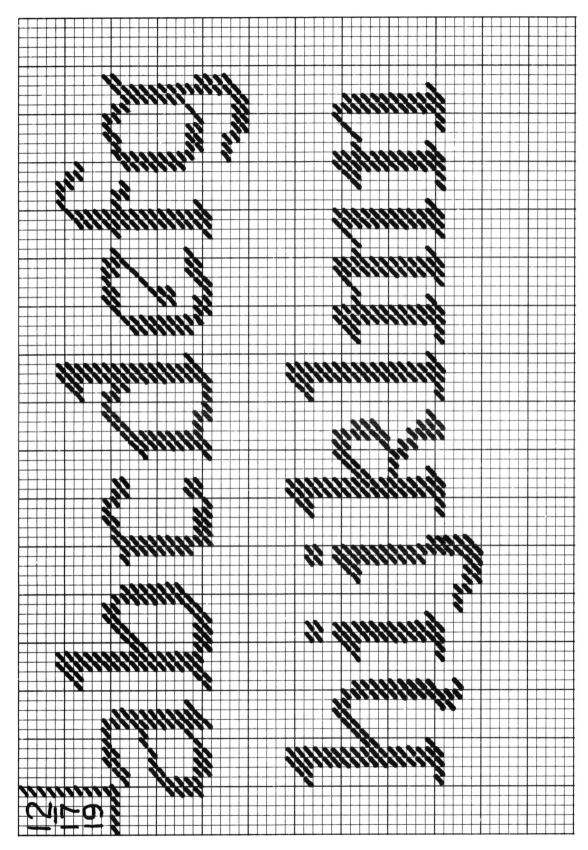

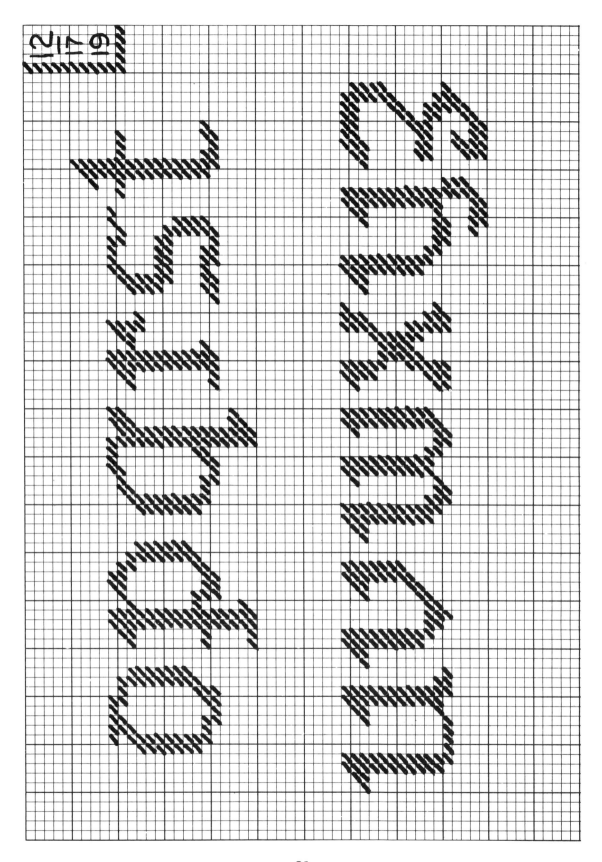

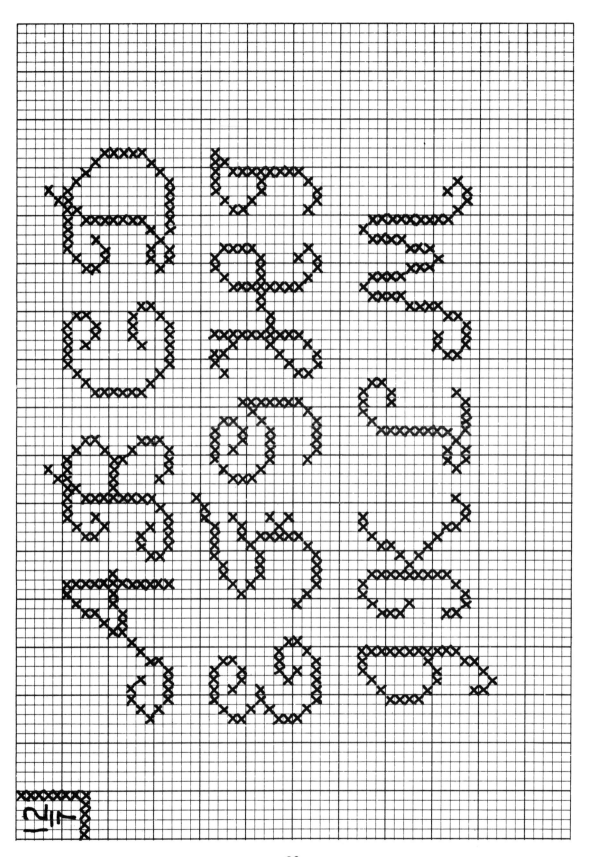

82

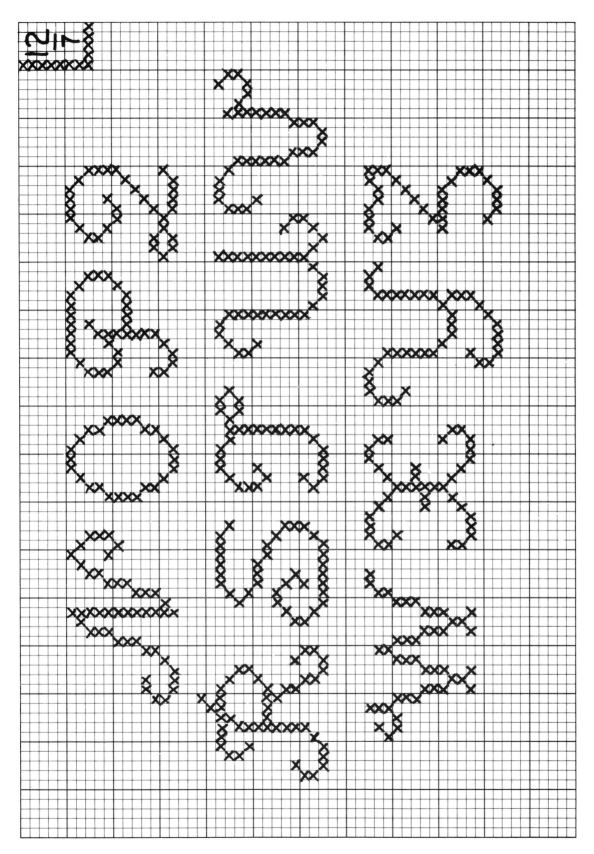

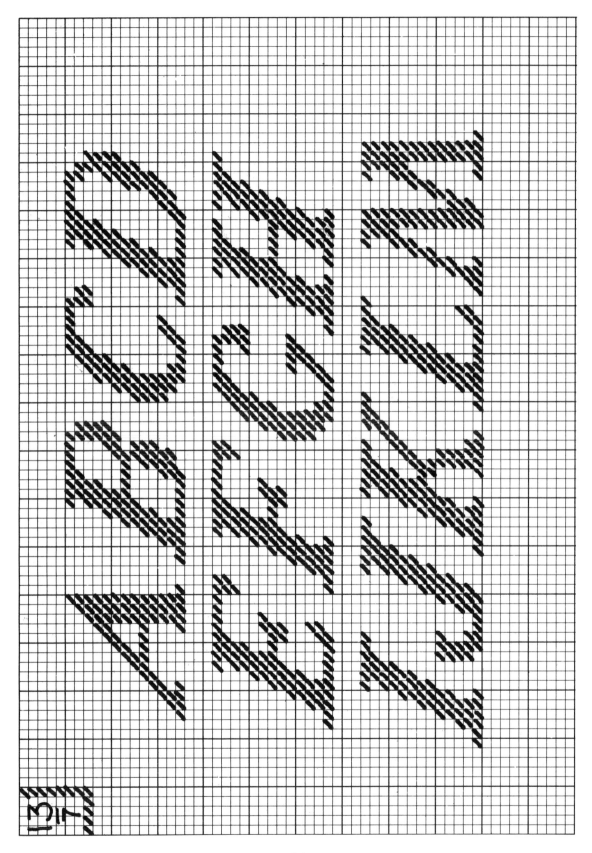

84

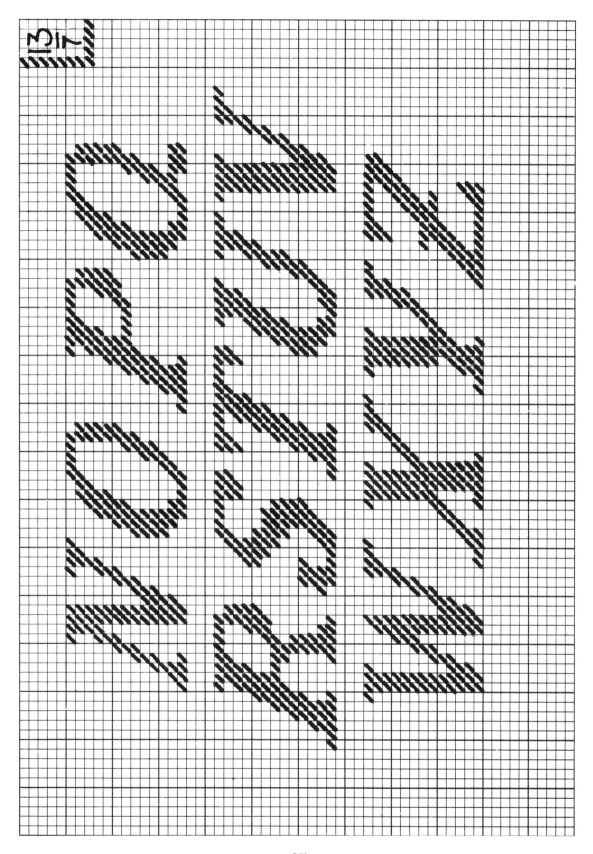

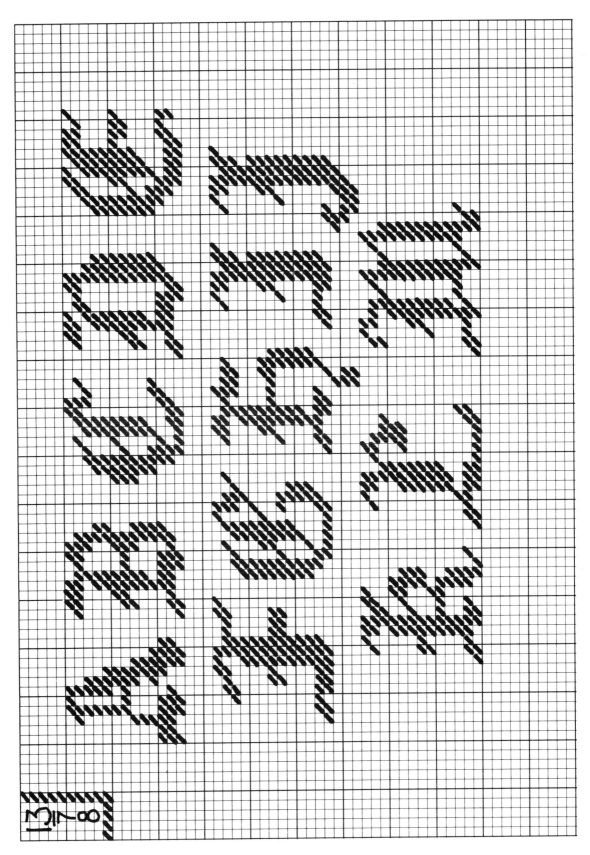

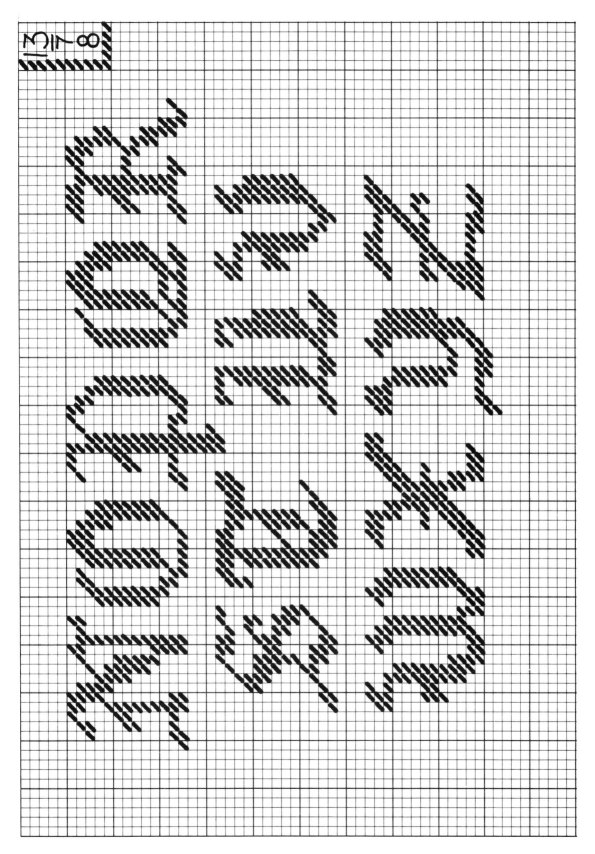

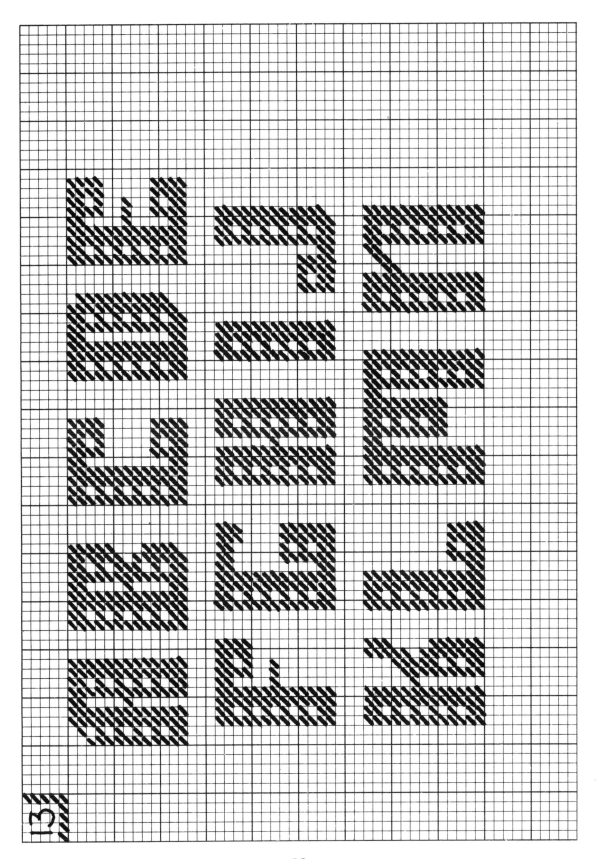

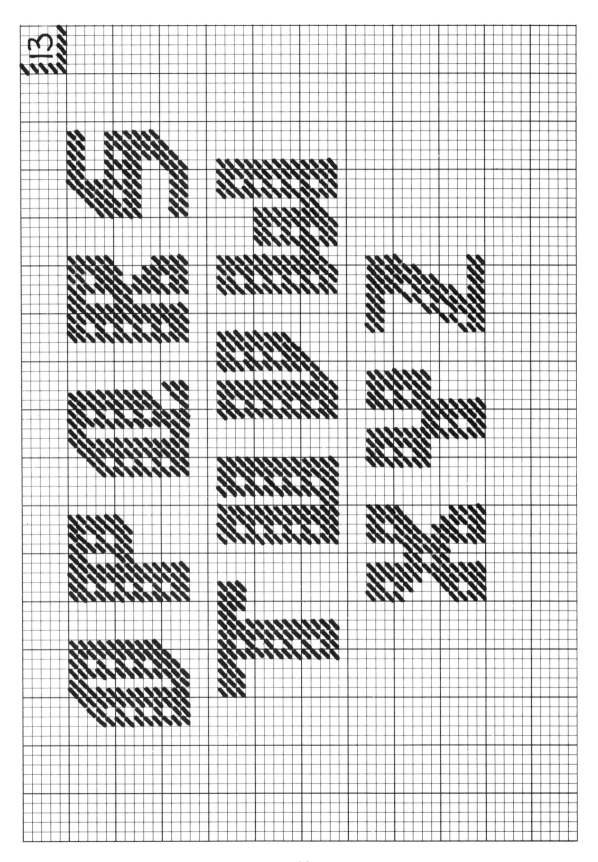

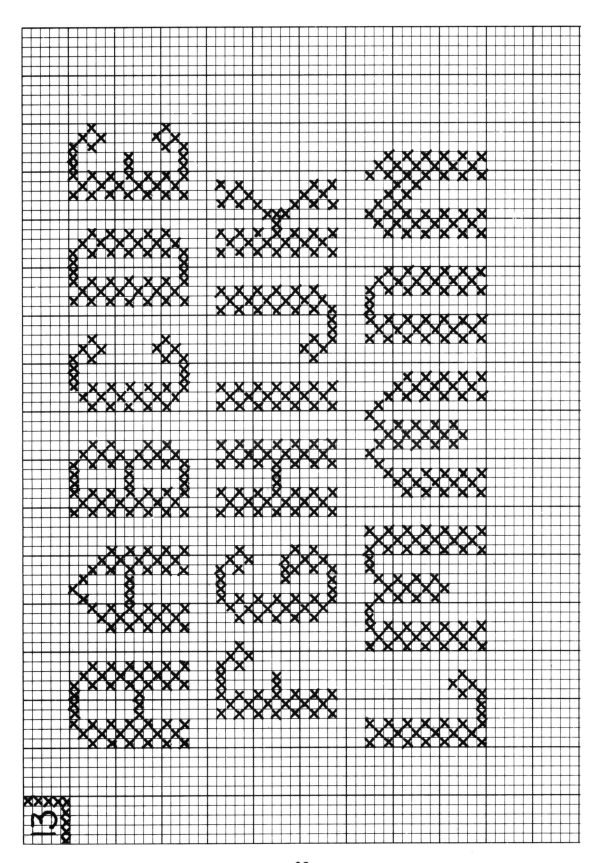

90

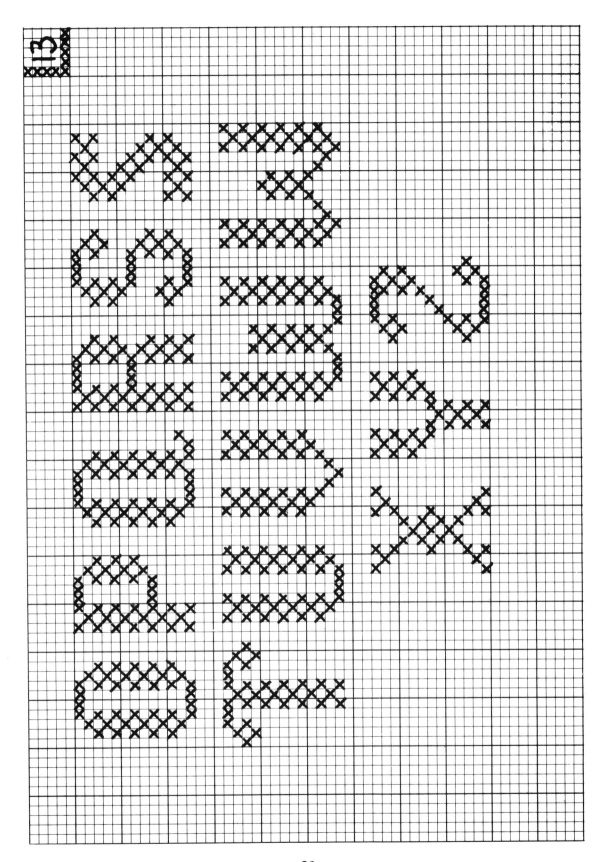

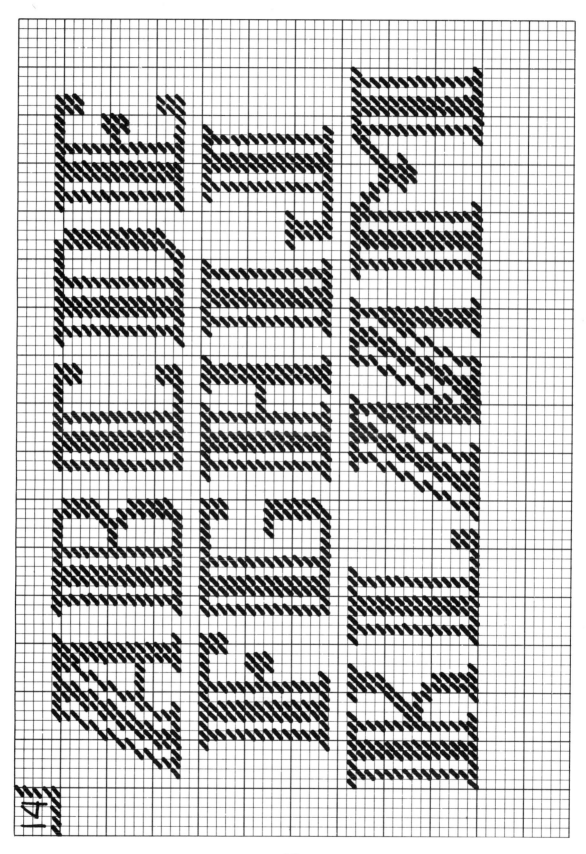

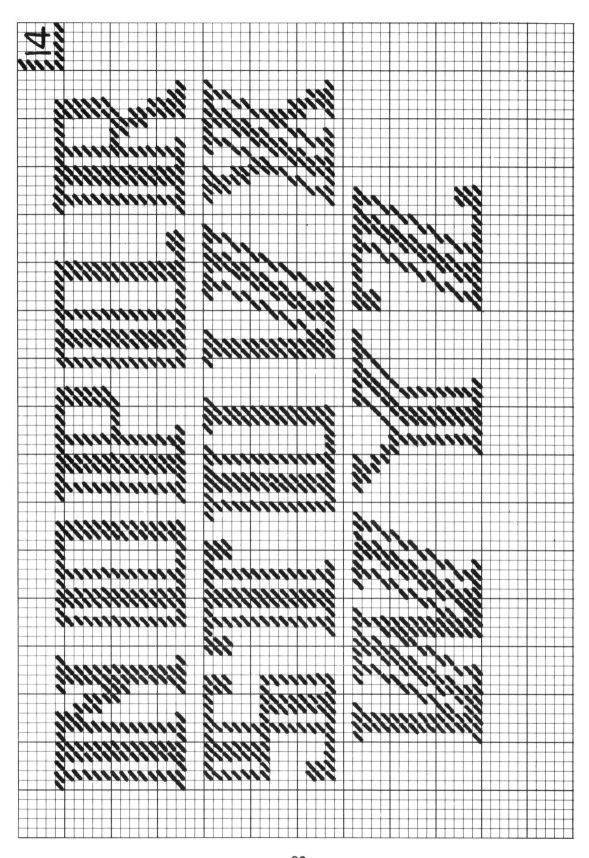

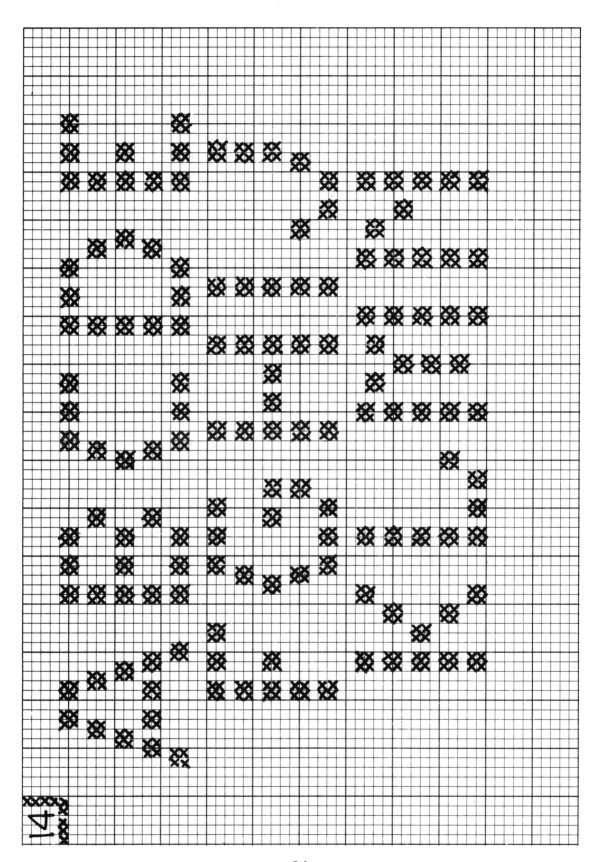

94

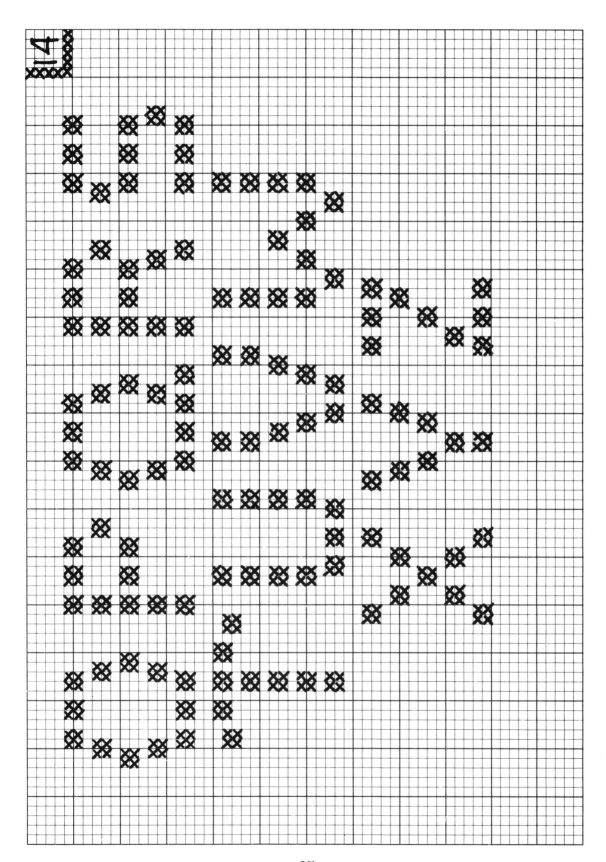

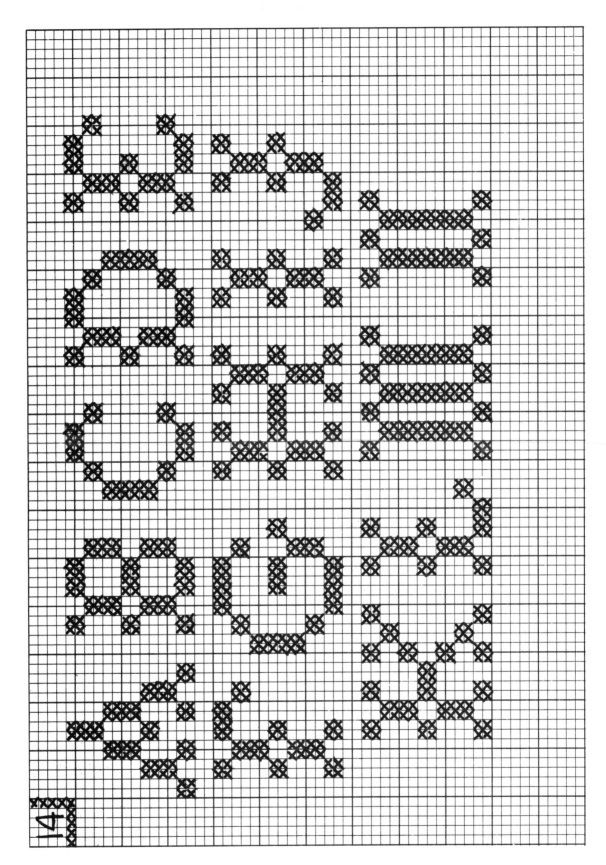

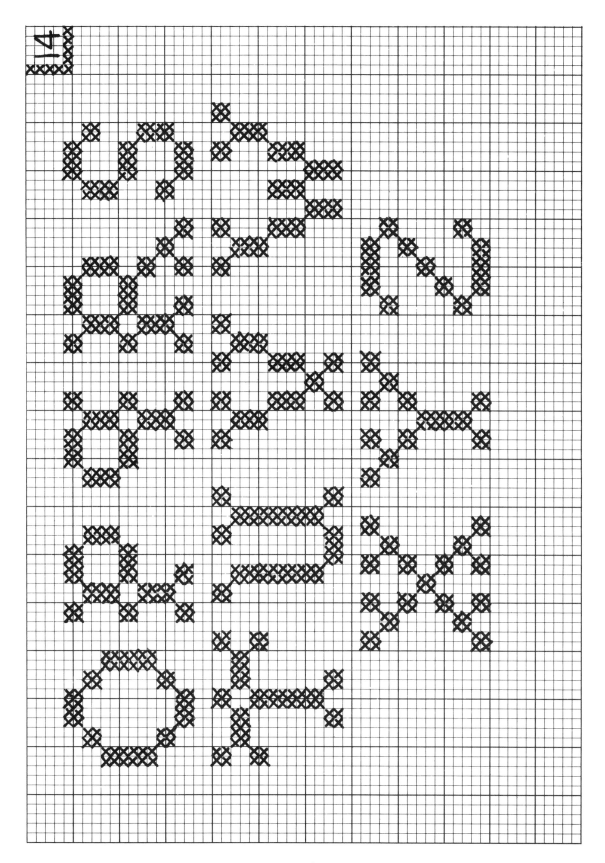

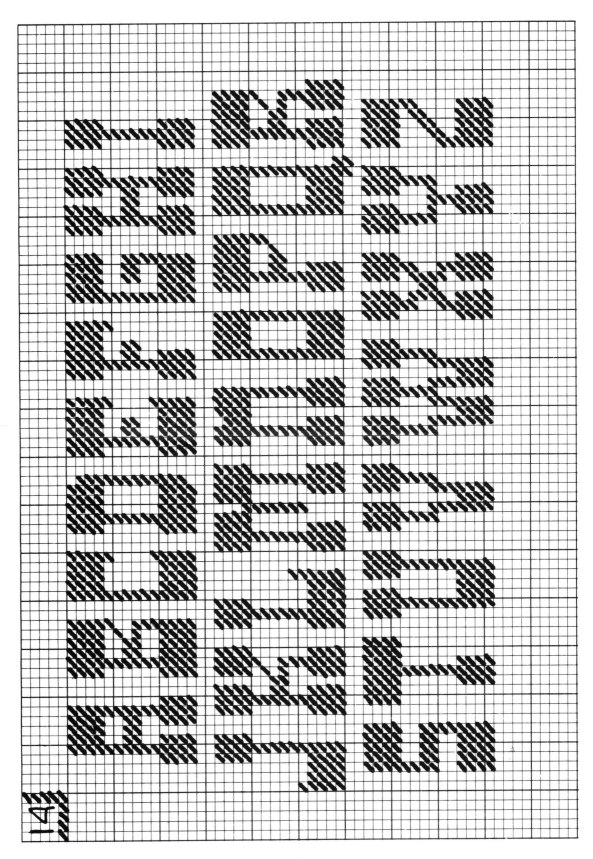

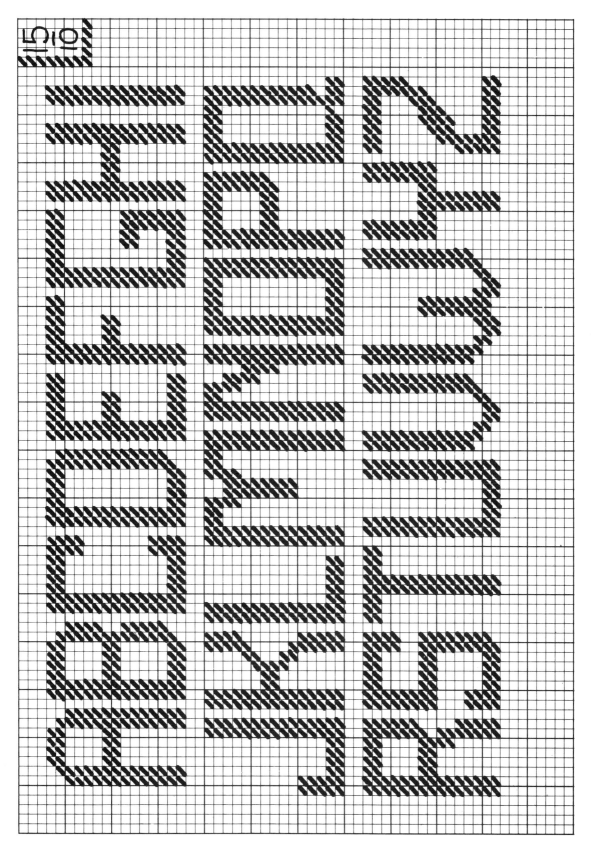

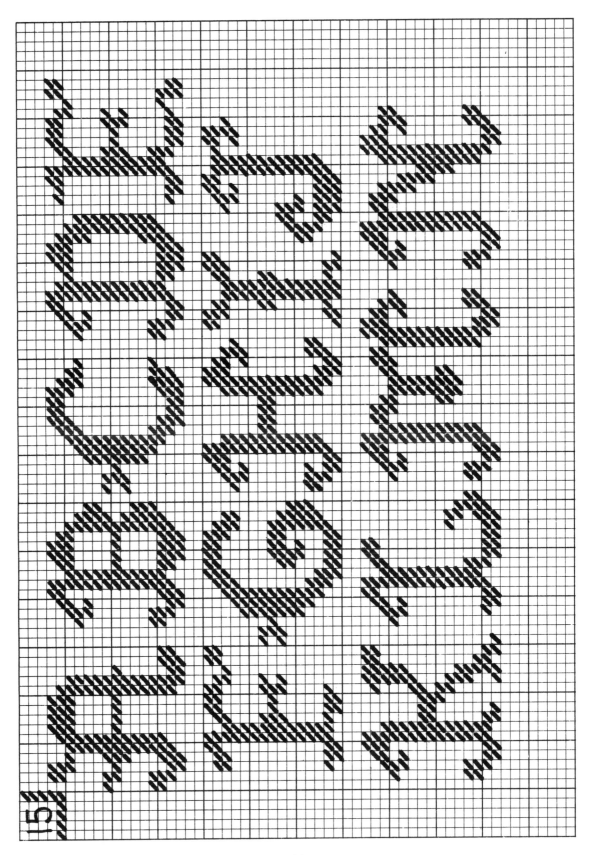

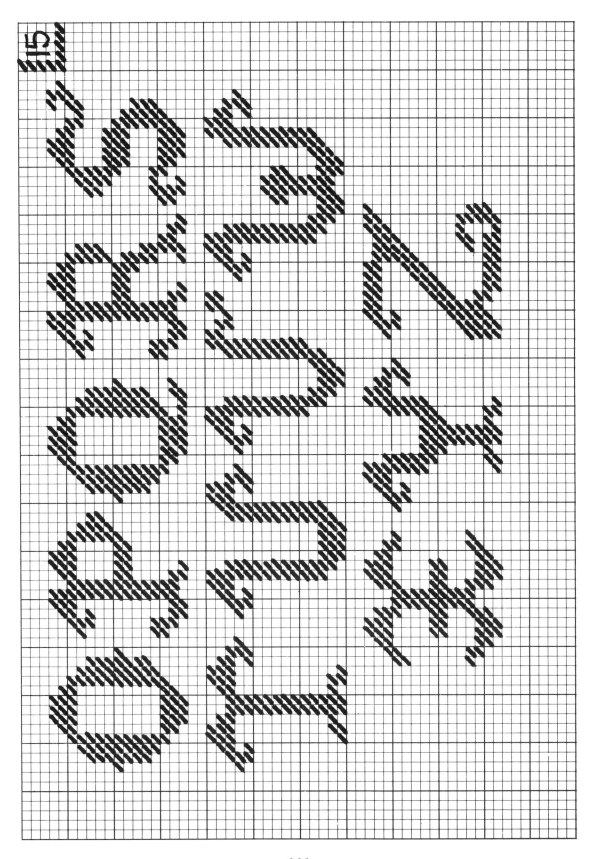

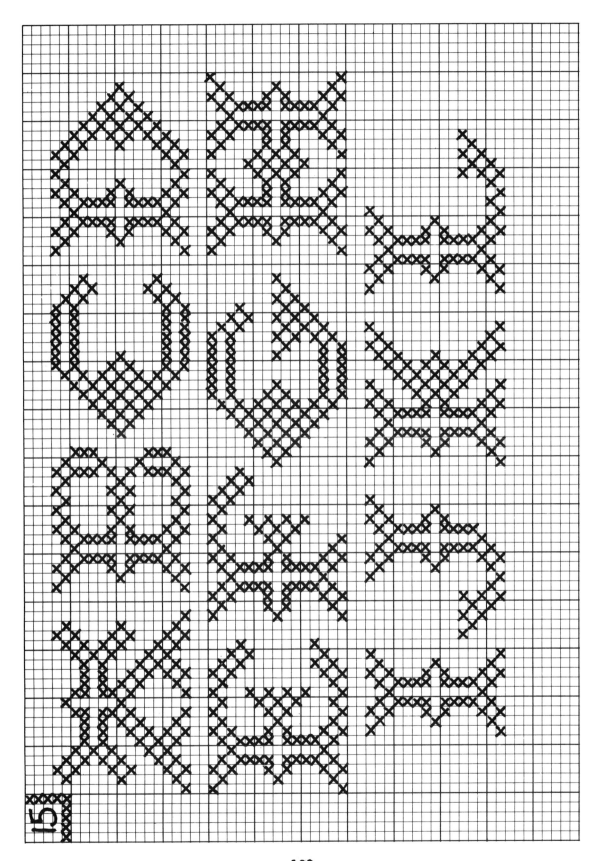

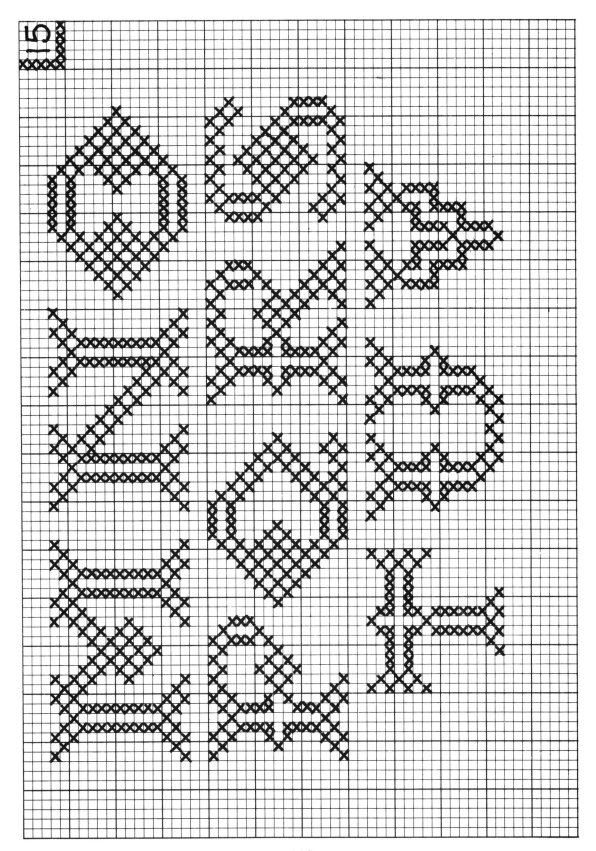

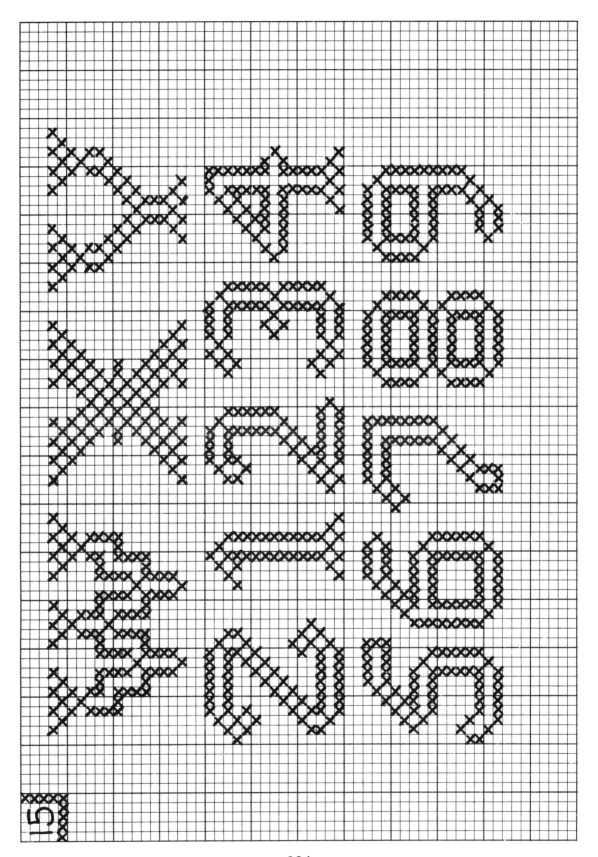

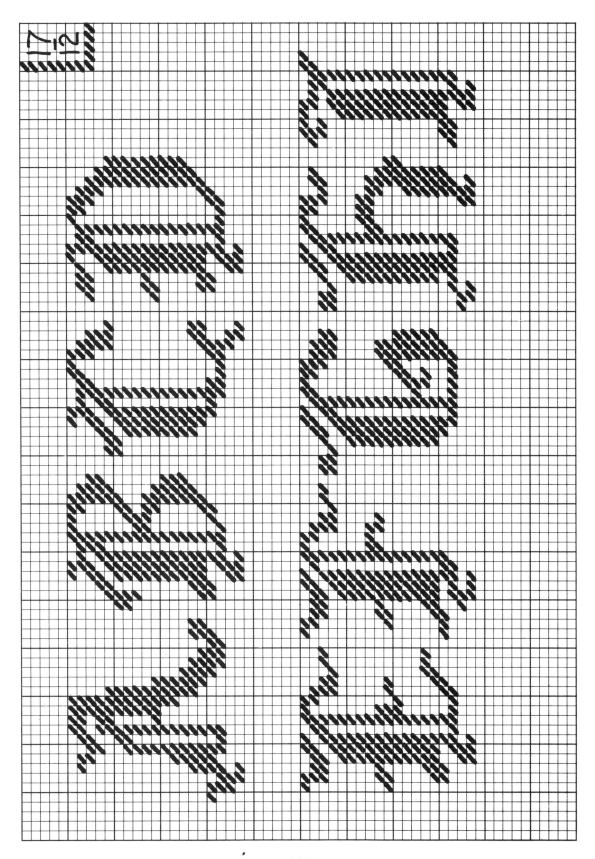

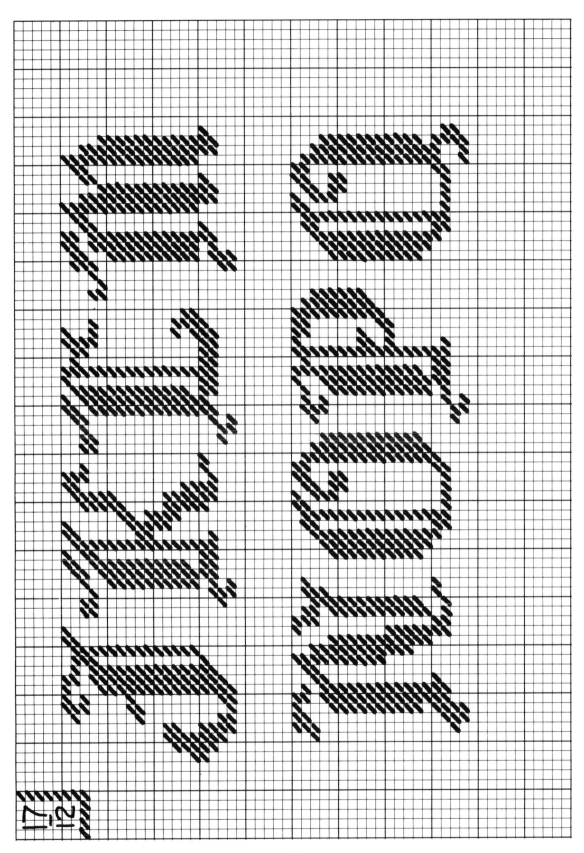

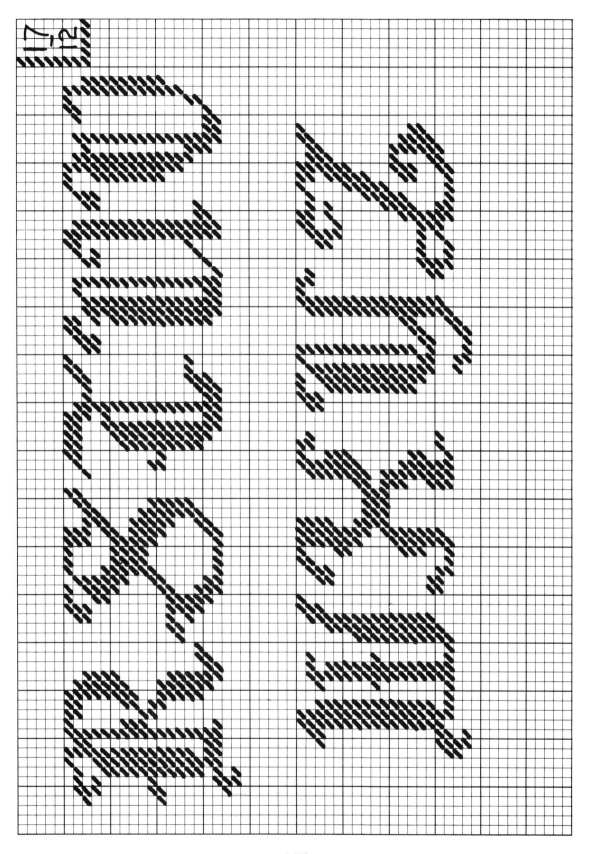

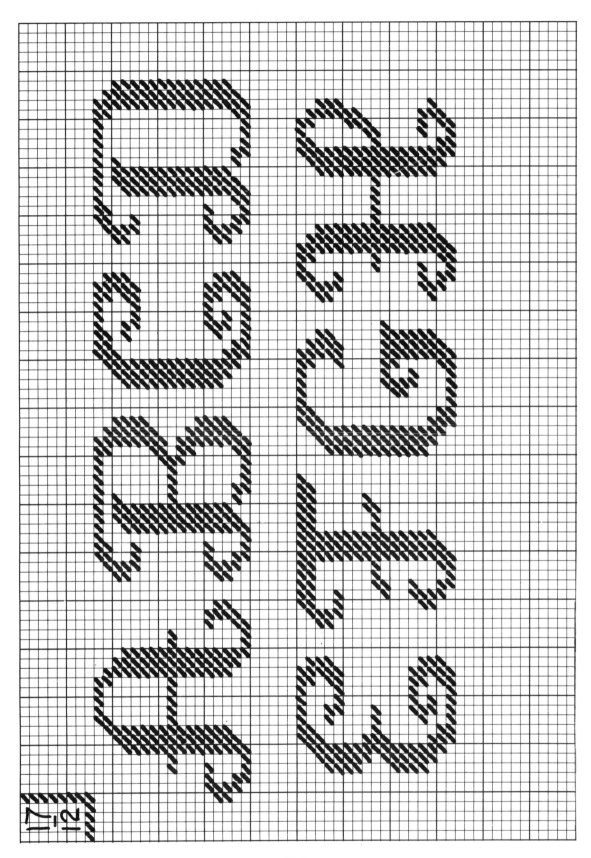

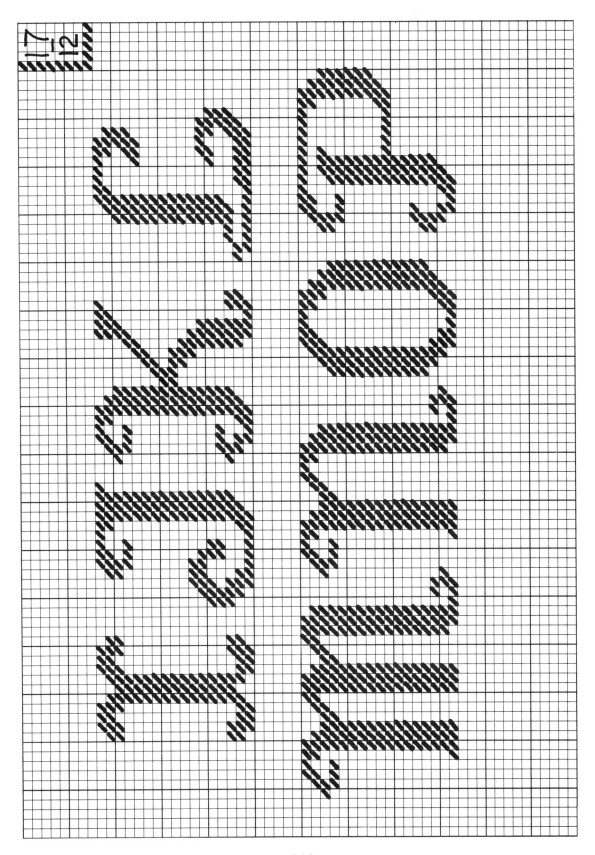

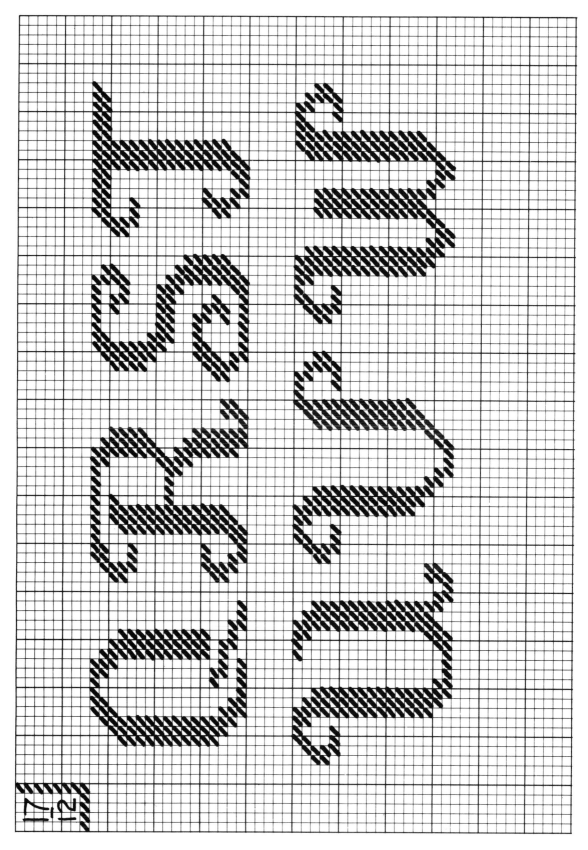

110

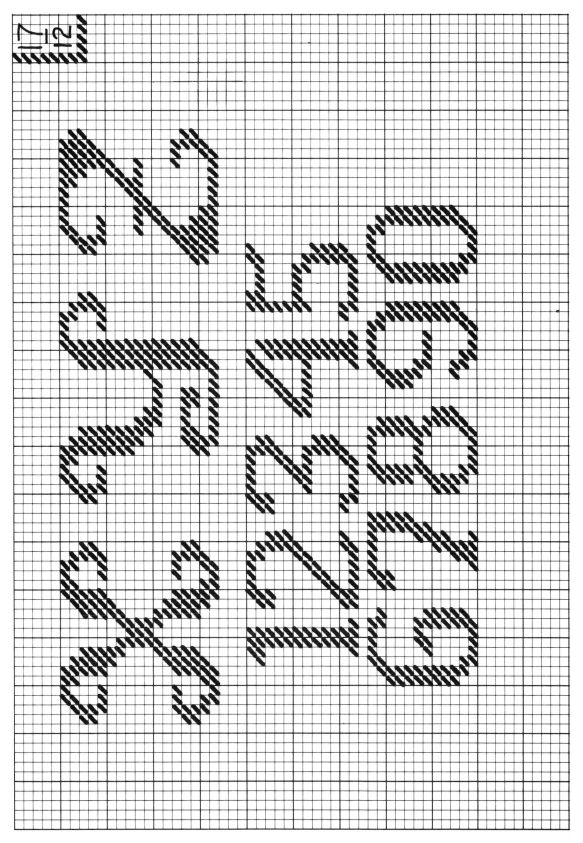

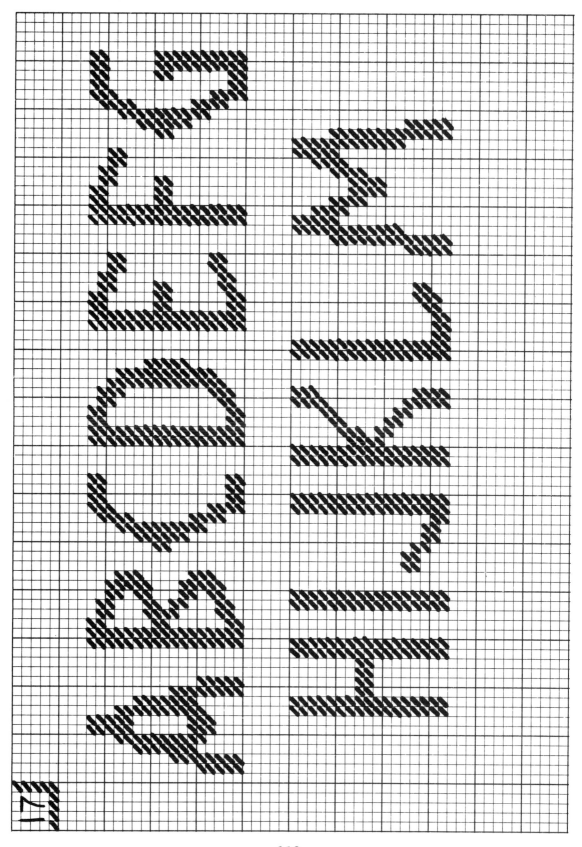

112

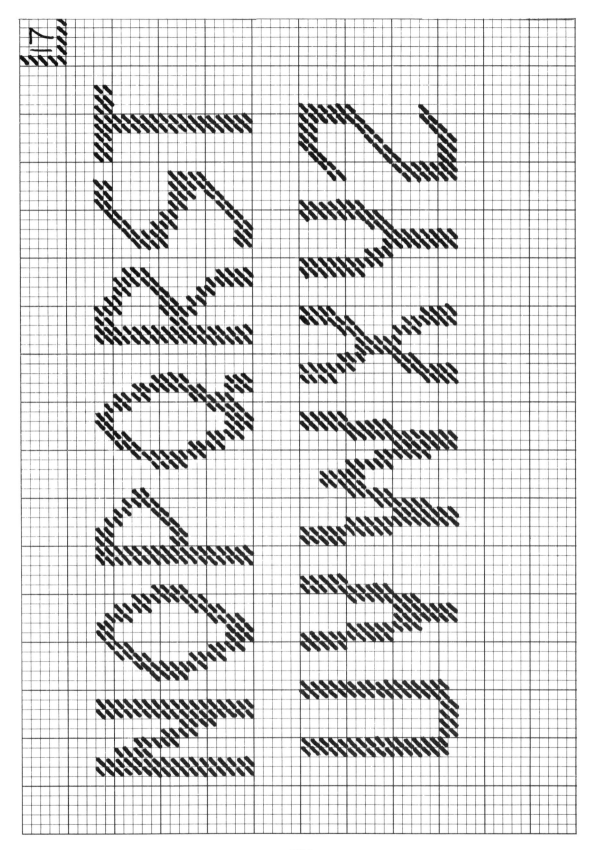

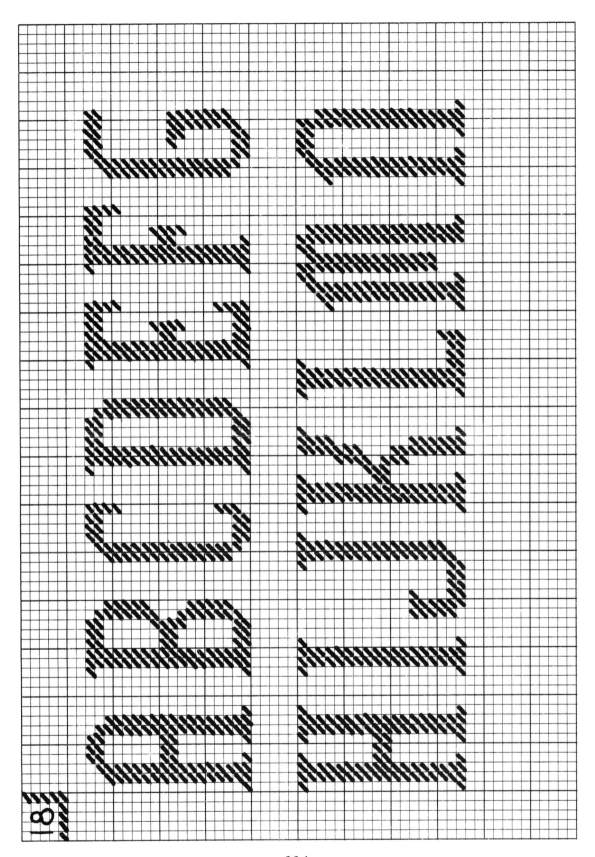

114

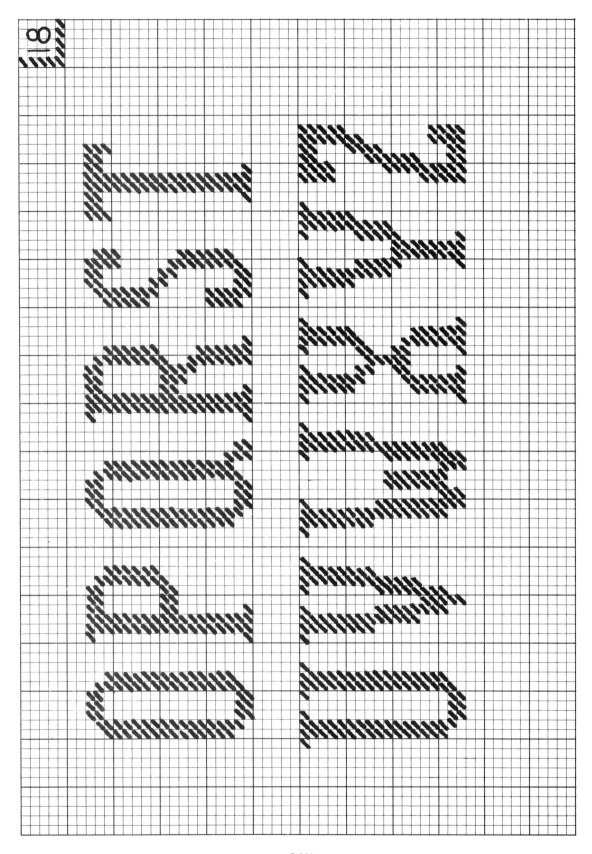

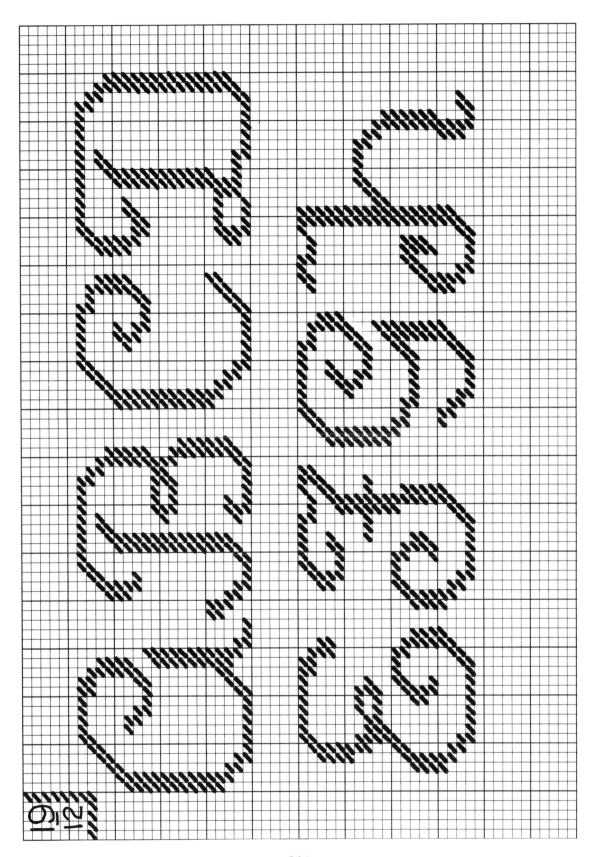

116

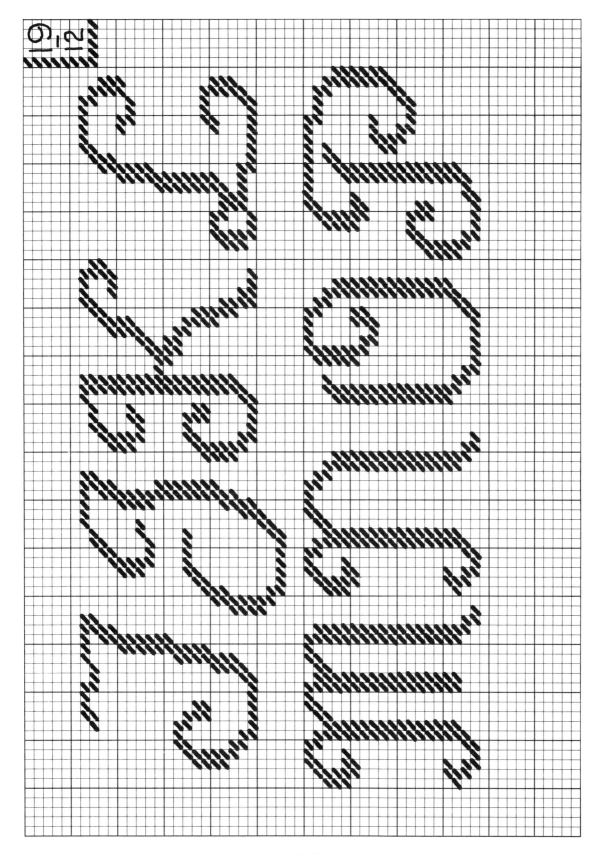

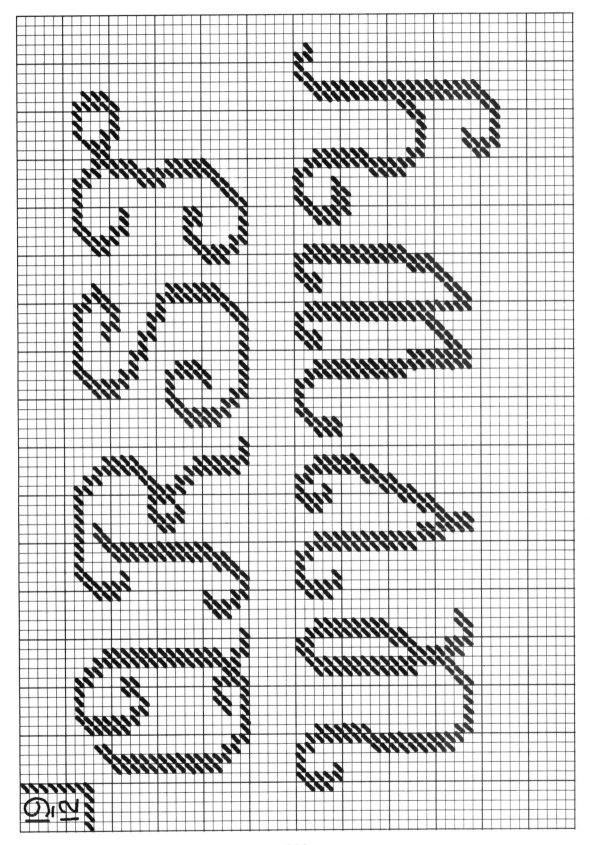

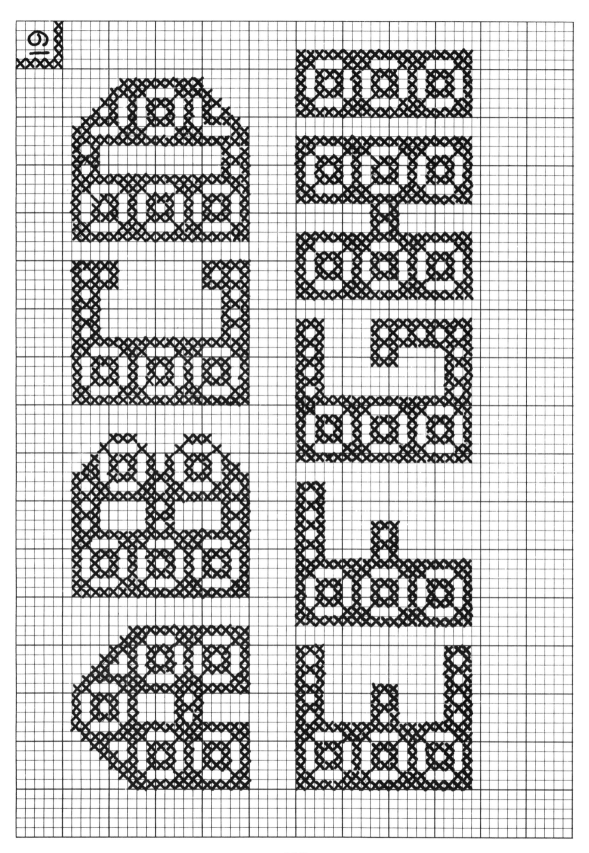

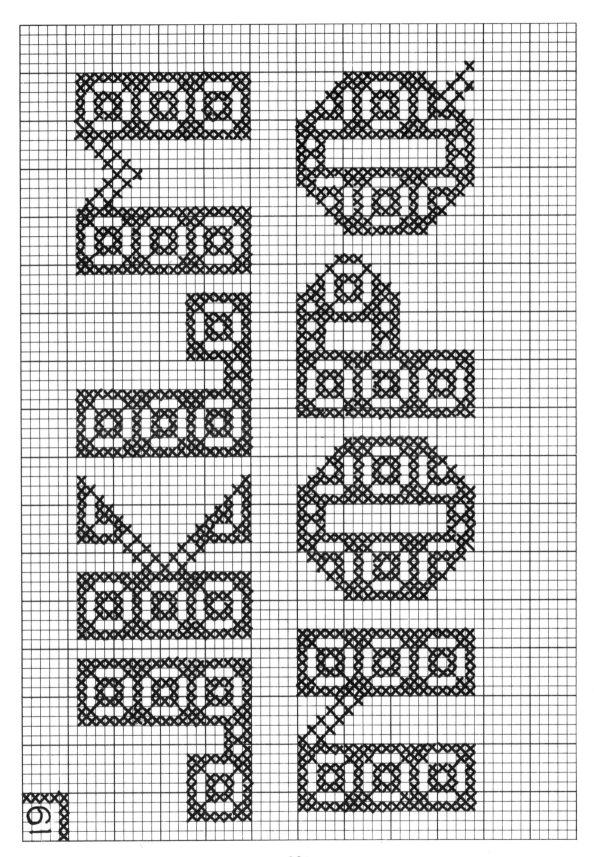

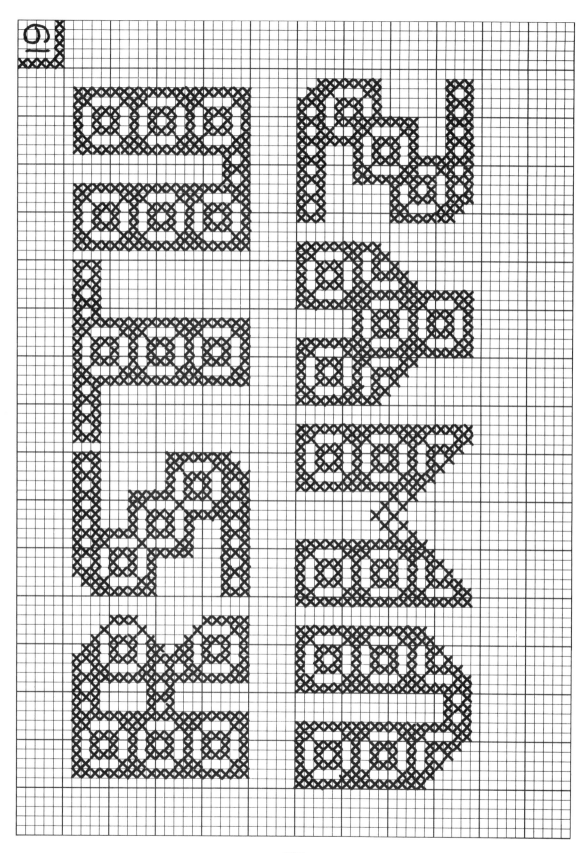

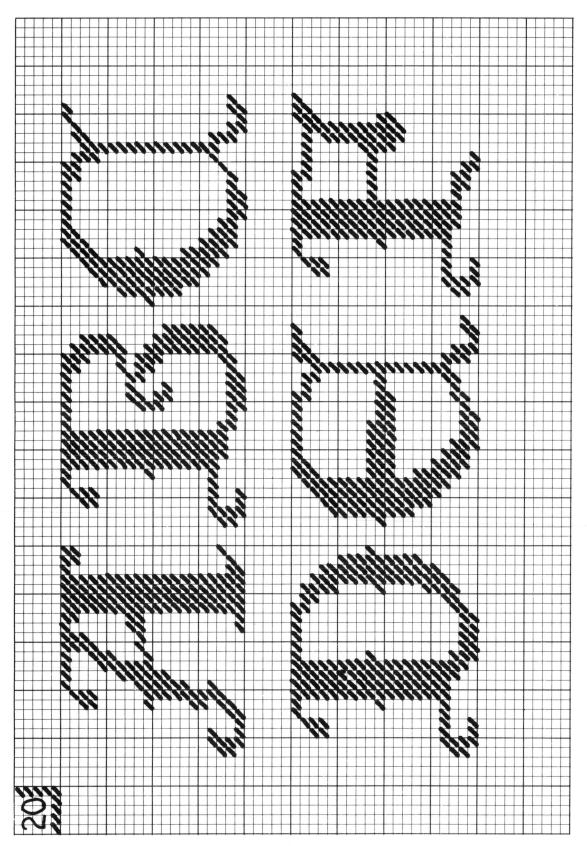

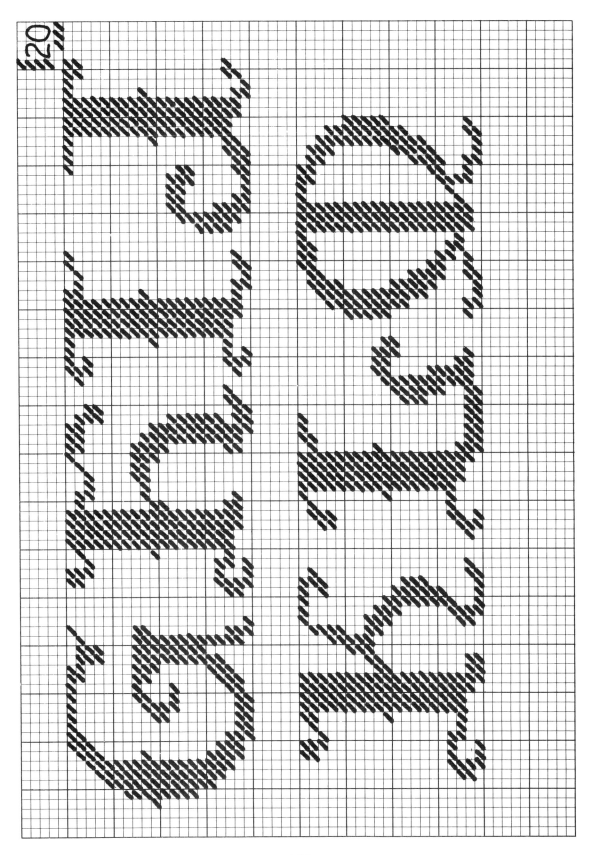

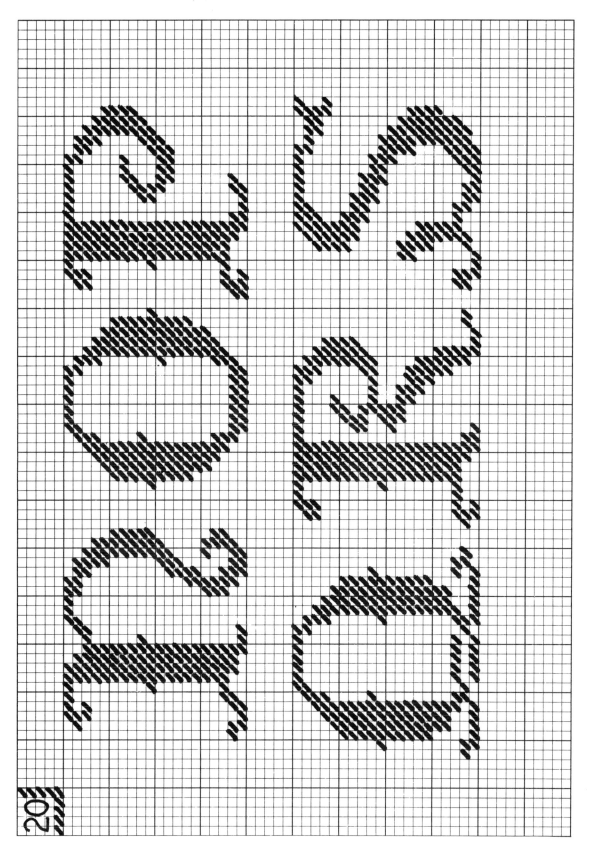

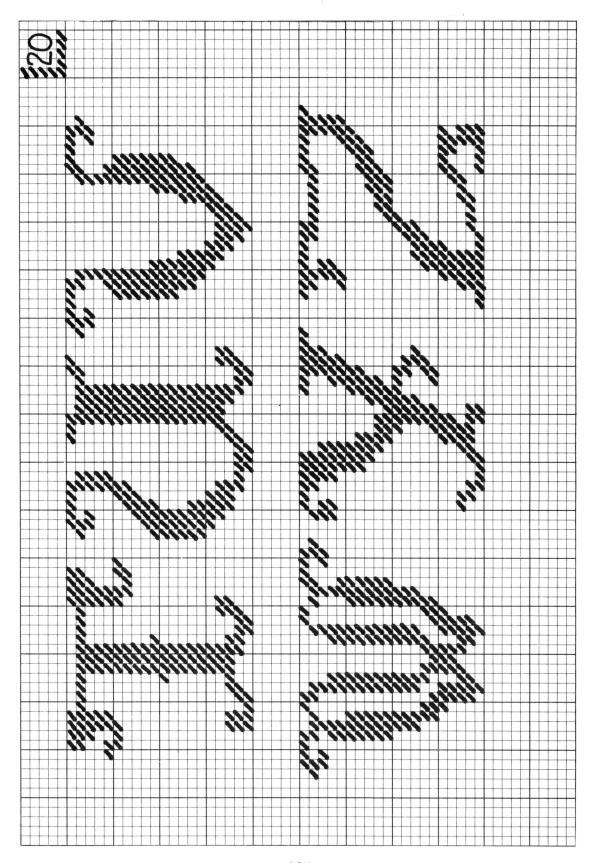

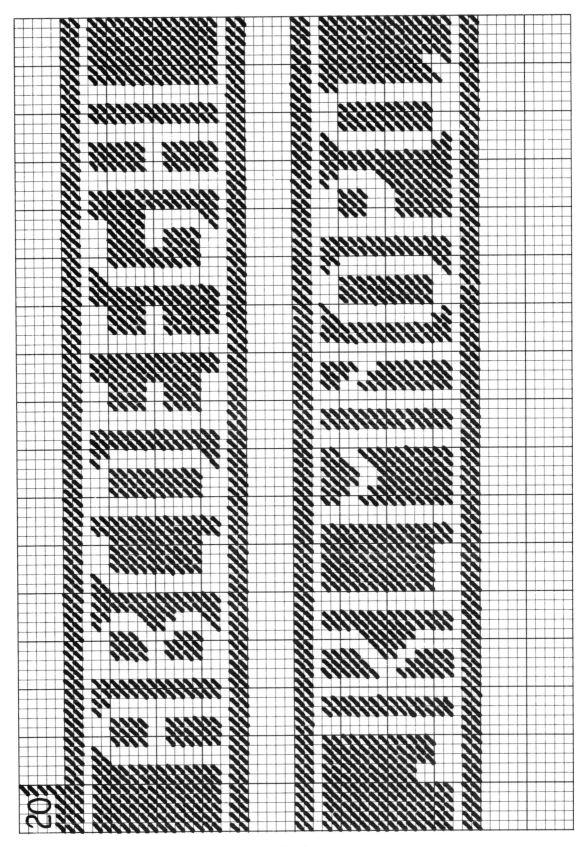

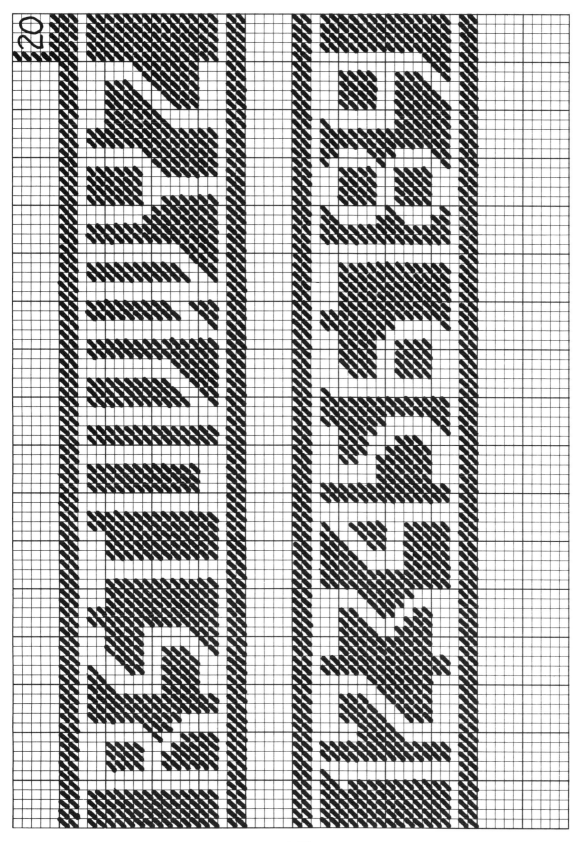

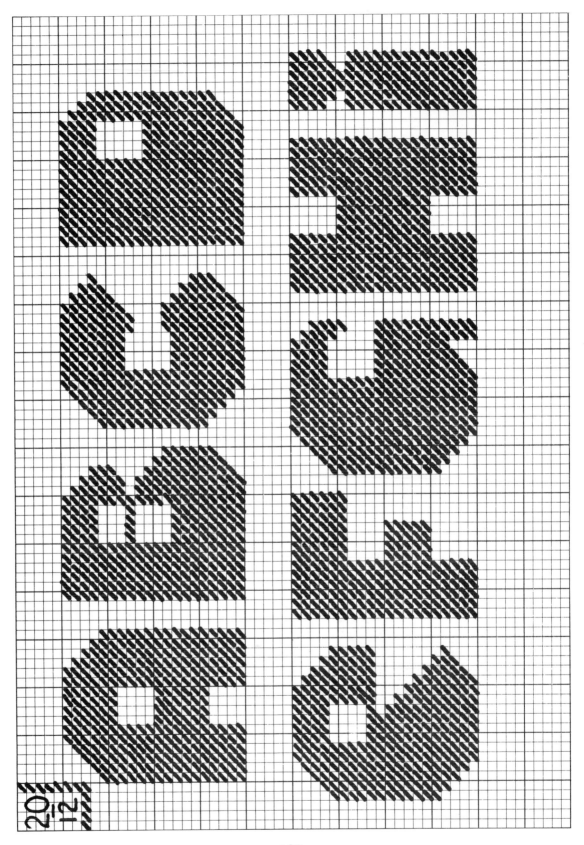

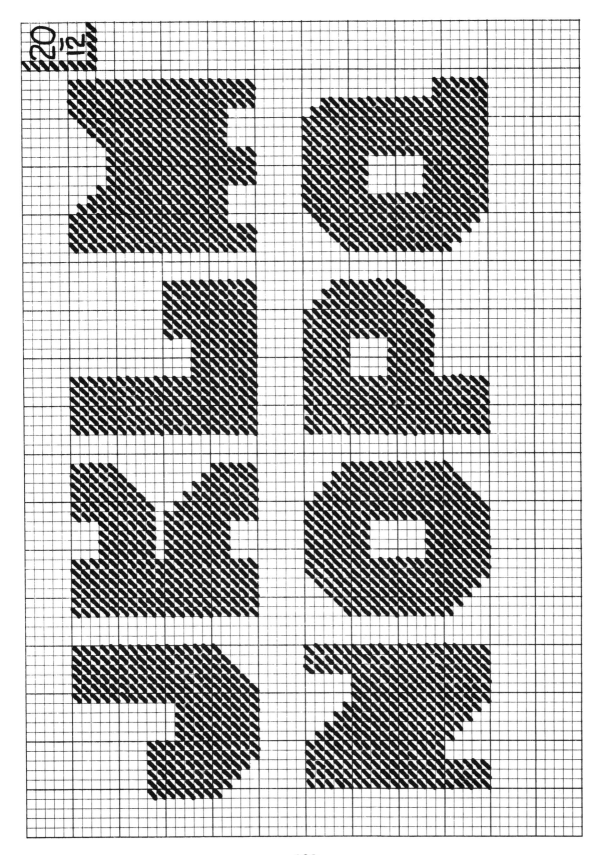

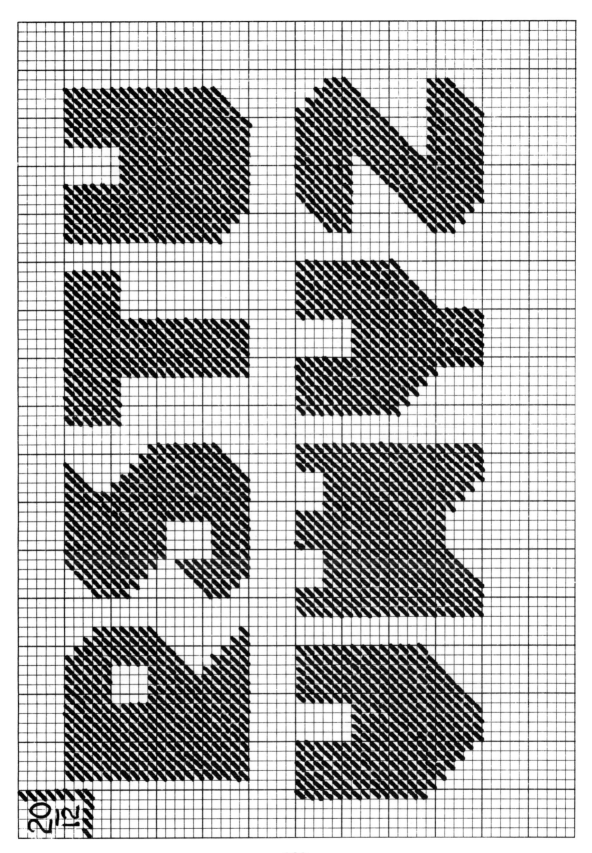

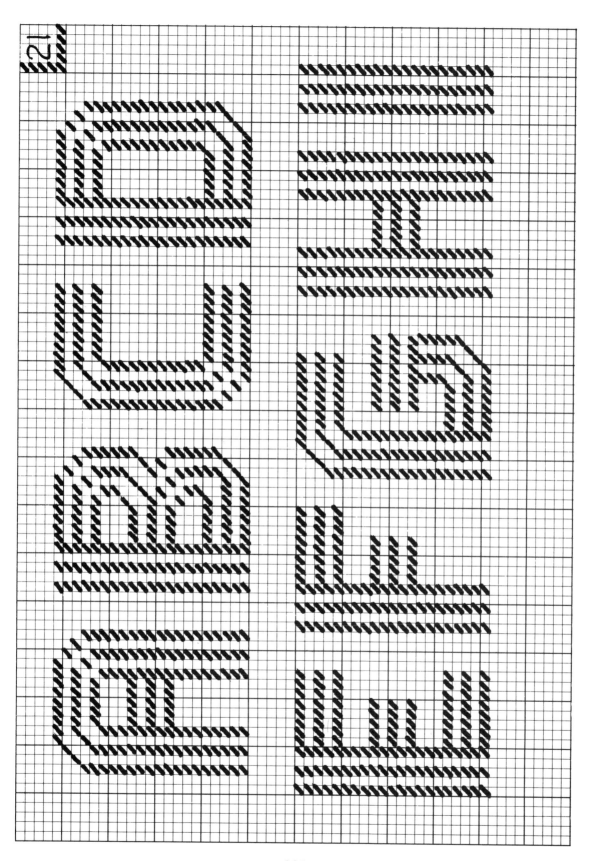

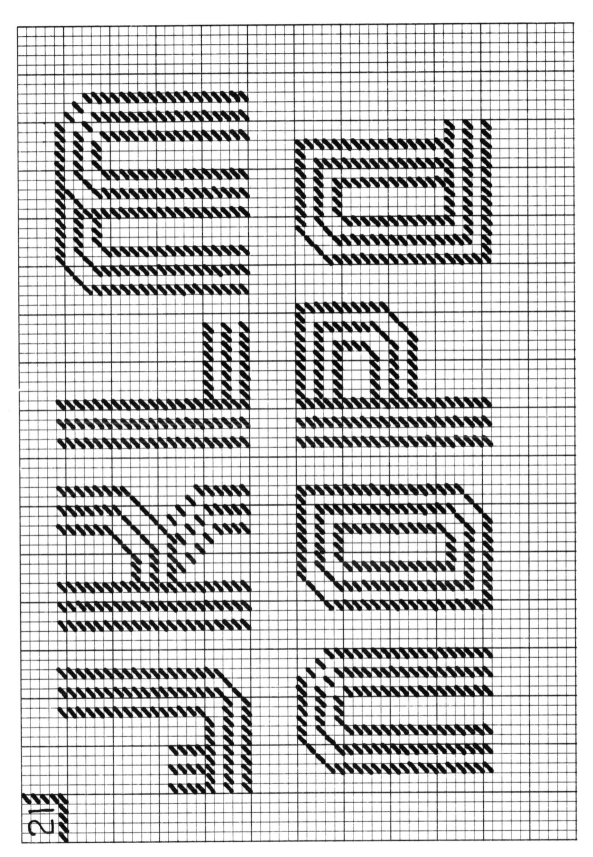

132

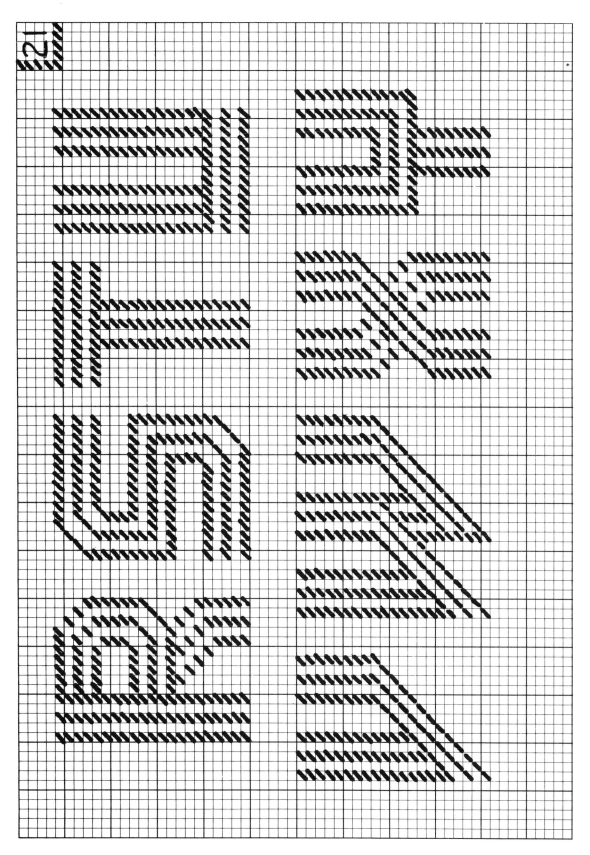

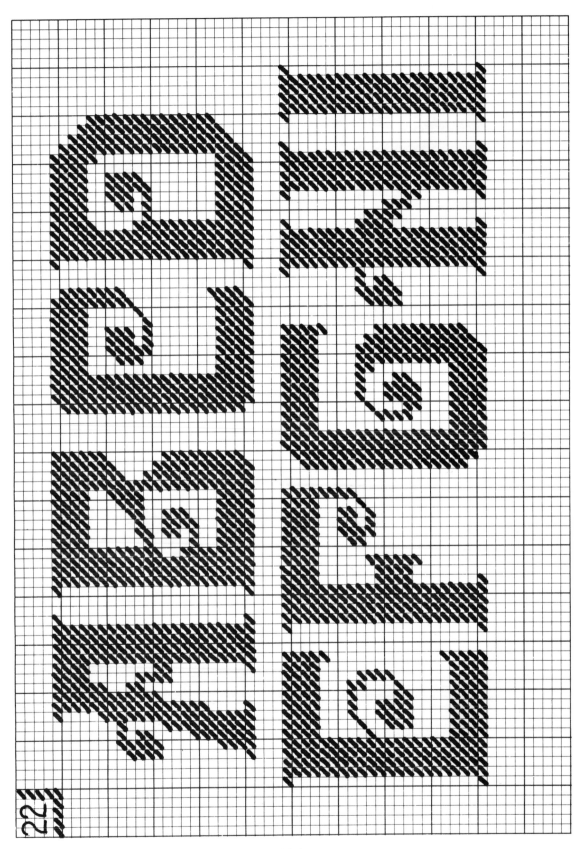

22

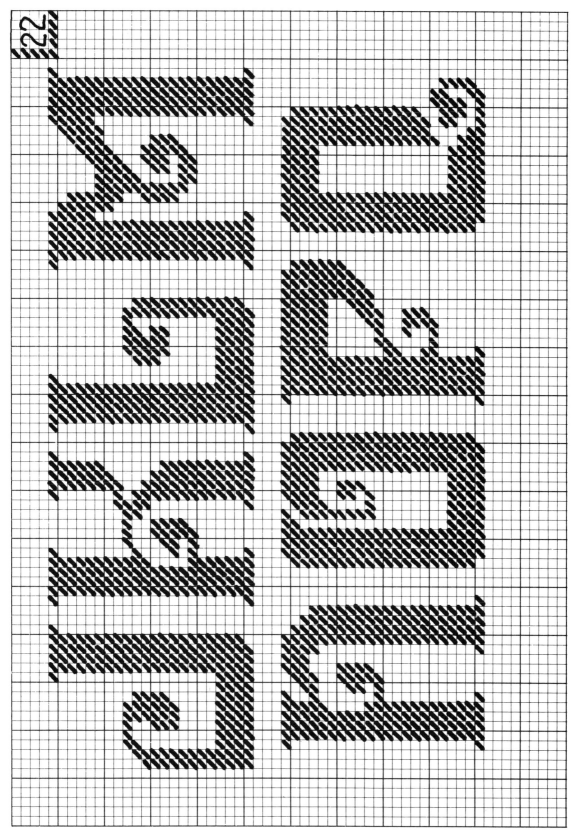

135

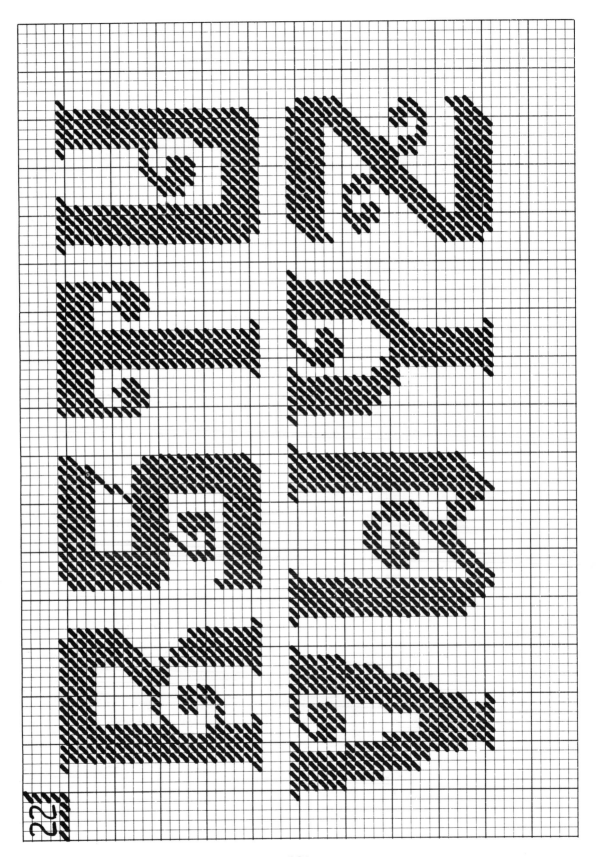

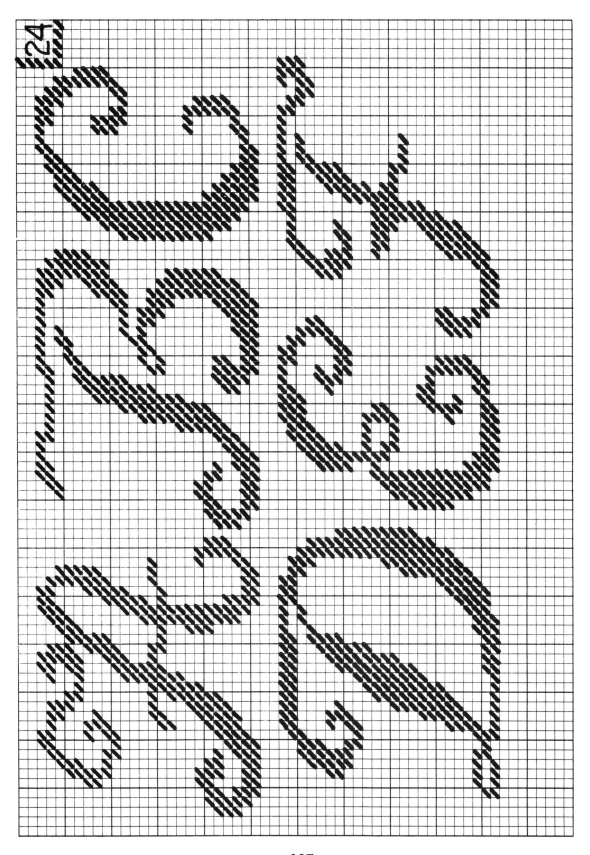

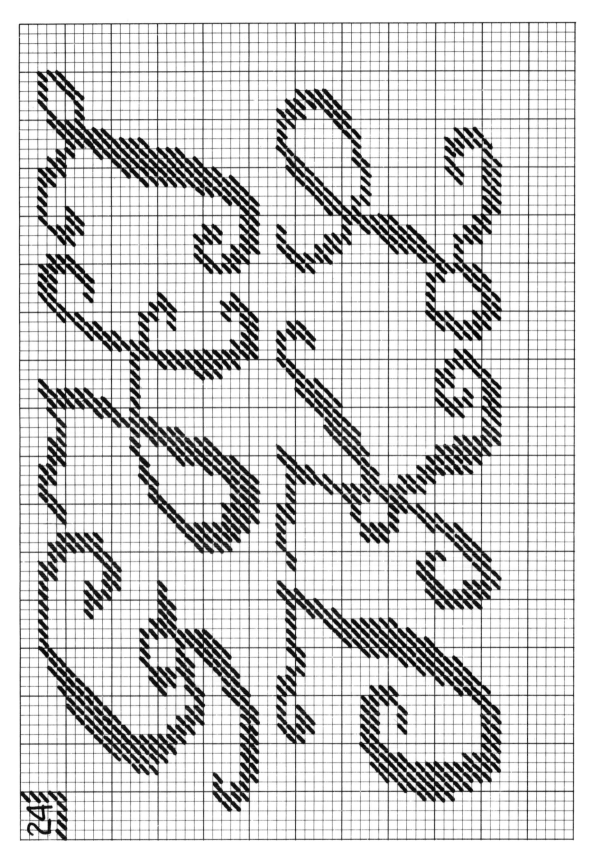

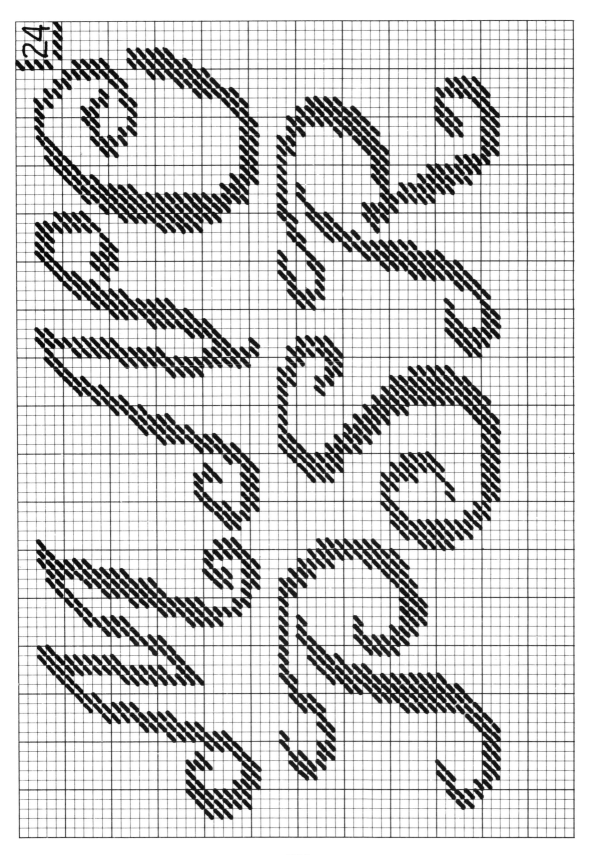

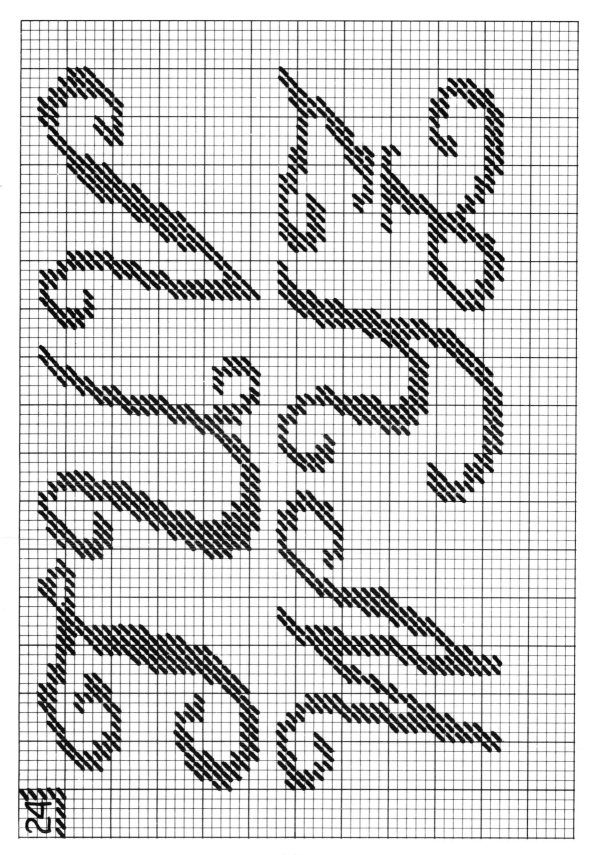

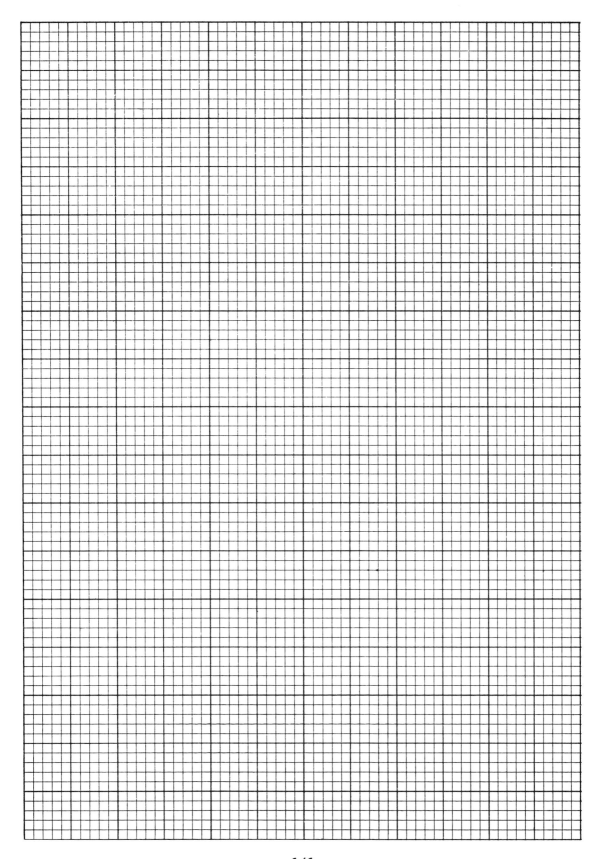

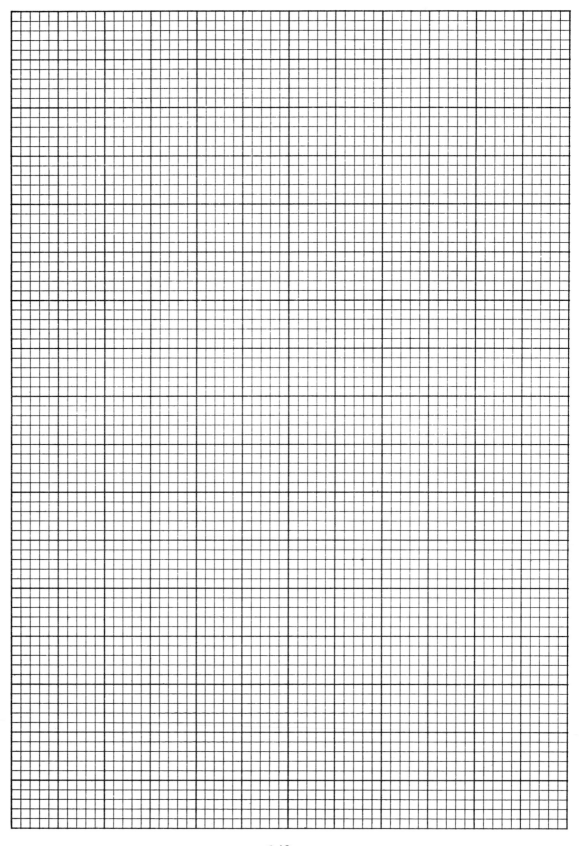

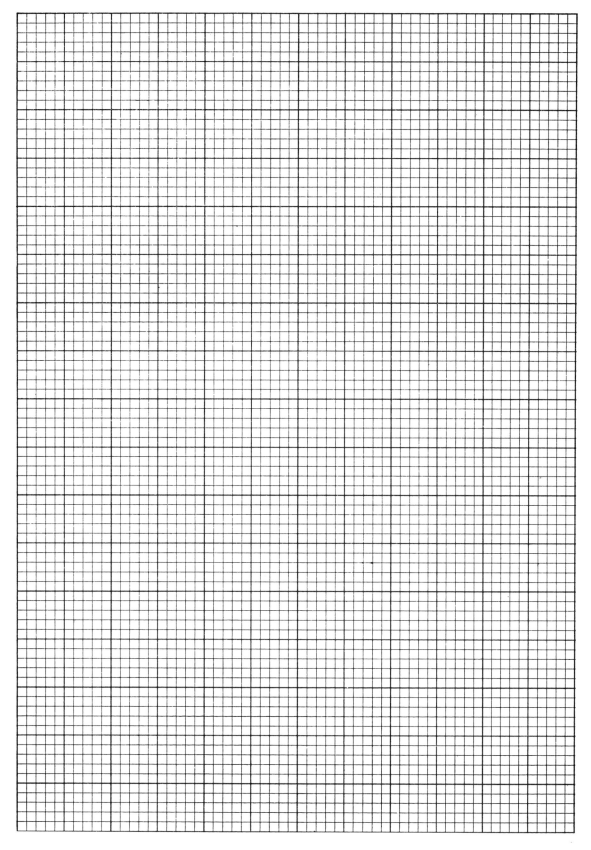

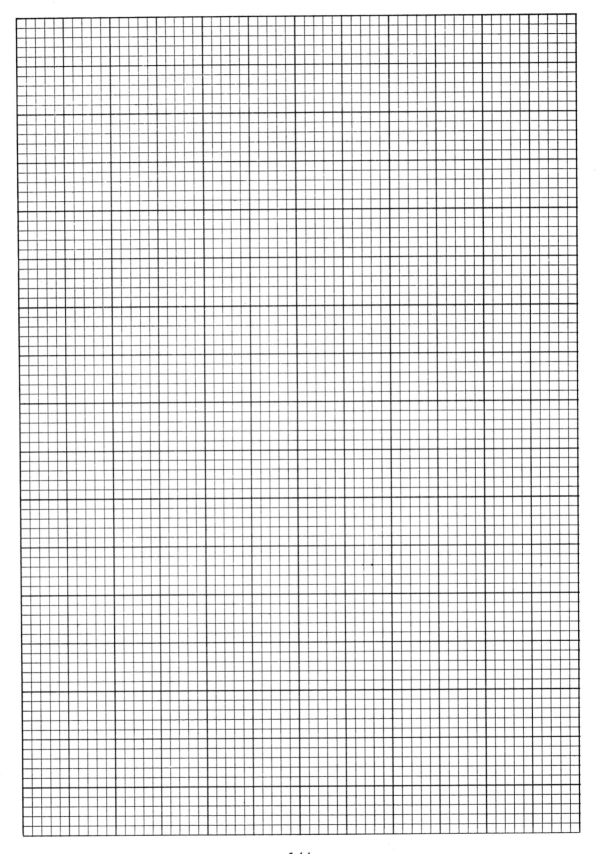